THE AUTHOR Robert Bothwell was born in Canada, educated at Harvard and is Professor of History at the University of Toronto. He has written many books, ranging from the problems of Atomic Energy to Canadian foreign relations.

SERIES EDITOR Professor Denis Judd is a graduate of Oxford, a Fellow of the Royal Historical Society and Professor of History at the University of North London. He has published over 20 books including biographies of Joseph Chamberlain, Prince Philip, George VI and Alison Uttley, historical and military subjects, stories for children and two novels. His most recent book is the highly praised *Empire: The British Imperial Experience from 1765 to the Present*. He has reviewed and written extensively in the national press and in journals, has written several radio programmes and is a regular contributor to British and overseas radio and television.

Other Titles in the Series

THE TRAVELLER'S HISTORY SERIES

A Traveller's History
of Canada

DEDICATION

For my wife Gail,
an indefatigable traveller and
purchaser of improving books.

Acknowledgements

I am most grateful to my research assistants, Tom Nevins, Serge Vucetic, Rutha Astravas and Mike Morgan, who sacrificed their tranquillity in the scrabble for data.

A Traveller's History
of Canada

Robert Bothwell

Series Editor   DENIS JUDD
Line Drawings   PETER GEISSLER

Interlink Books
An imprint of Interlink Publishing Group, Inc.
New York • Northampton

First American edition published in 2002 by
INTERLINK BOOKS
An imprint of Interlink Publishing Group, Inc.
99 Seventh Avenue • Brooklyn, New York 11215 and
46 Crosby Street • Northampton, Massachusetts 01060

*The front cover shows 'Indians transporting furs through the Canadian wilderness' 1858
by Cornelius Krieghoff. By permission of the Bridgeman Art Library*

Library of Congress Cataloging-in-Publication Data

Bothwell, Robert.
    A traveller's history of Canada/Robert Bothwell.–1st American ed.
       p. cm.–(The traveller's history)
    Includes bibliographical references and index.
    ISBN 1-56656-386-0
    1. Canada–History. 2. Canada–Description and travel. I. Title. II. Series.

  F1026 .B75 2001
  971–dc21

                                00-053890

Printed and bound in Great Britain

To order or request our complete catalog,
please call us at **1–800–238–LINK** or write to:
Interlink Publishing
46 Crosby Street, Northampton, MA 01060
e-mail: info@interlinkbooks.com • website: www.interlinkbooks.com

Table of Contents

Preface

Canada is the second largest country in the world. It is, however, comparatively sparsely populated, and the vast majority of its people live either near the coast or along the 3000 mile border with the United States. Only 3 per cent of Canadian land is usable for arable farming, and in the far north the permanent grip of ice means that nothing can grow there. Ottawa is the world's coldest capital city after Mongolia's Ulan Bator. All of these surprising facts can be found in the early pages of Robert Bothwell's fascinating, accomplished and remarkably comprehensive book.

As with certain other countries, it may be tempting to describe Canada as more of a geographical expression than a well-integrated and coherent state. Such a judgement would, however, be a glib and trite dismissal of a land with a clear and well-documented history and a well-developed sense of national identity. It has, it is true, taken Canada some time to emerge from the shadow of its over-mighty neighbour the United States, and to disentangle itself from its umbilical imperial link with Britain. Bismarck once predicted that the twenty-first century would belong to Canada, just as the twentieth would be dominated by the United States, and although he has yet to be proved right in the case of Canada, it was an intriguing and daring prophesy.

The first human settlements in Canada date from 20,000 years ago, well before the retreat of the ice that left the country with its present climate and topography. The first European contact was about one thousand years ago when Norse settlers landed on the northern coast of Newfoundland. After their failure to establish a permanent presence it was left to the ambitions of the first Tudor king, Henry VII, to finance the 1497 expedition of John Cabot to Newfoundland. Four decades later, the Frenchman Jacques Cartier laid claim to territory that was to introduce the second European Mother Country to Canadian history.

Until the crushing British victory in the Seven Years' War of 1756–63 it was not clear whether Britain or France would dominate North America – despite the preponderance of English-speaking settlers in the continent, one and a half million by the mid-1750s as opposed to a mere 55,000 French-speakers. Even after the incorporation of New France into the British Empire, Britain was careful to respect the religious and linguistic identity of Quebec in a shrewd move calculated to secure the long-term future of its new possession.

The nineteenth century saw Canadian colonies lead the way in the establishment of self-governing institutions within the empire. The confederation of British North America was achieved in 1867, and the Dominion of Canada was born. Determined not to become another state within the increasingly powerful United States, Canada, supported by Britain, went out of its way to assert its separate identity. One device was to build the Canadian Pacific Railway as a practical link that emphasised the east-west nature of Canada's character rather than the north-south connections with the United States.

By the beginning of the twentieth century, Canada was the senior Dominion within the British Empire, and in Kipling's verse 'daughter in my mother's house, but mistress in my own.' As the population and prosperity of Canada grew, the domination of the country's English-speakers was consolidated. The capacity of Quebec to rock the boat was given expression in the development of the separatist movement and at moments of crisis, as in the First World War when rioters protested against the attempt to introduce military conscription. The confederation survived, however, and went on to play a less ambiguous part in the Second World War.

Today Canada is a mature, self-confident country, proud of its pluralism and welcoming towards the new immigrants of the 1980s and 90s, many of them from Asia and the Caribbean. The French-speakers seem reconciled to their role in a united and successful country. The Canadian Health Service is a model to other nations. Capitalism and social welfare seem at ease with each other. Canadian authors like

Margaret Atwood and Carol Shields write bestsellers that are eagerly bought not merely within the English-speaking world, but well beyond it. No longer is the Mountie the stereotypical symbol of a barely recognised country.

Each year thousands of tourists and holidaymakers flood into Canada from overseas, anxious to sample the sophisticated pleasures of Quebec and Montreal, to experience the big city bustle of Toronto, to admire the coast of British Columbia, to see the plains of Alberta and Saskatchewan, or to enjoy the countryside and maritime pastimes of Nova Scotia and Prince Edward Island. For these visitors, this concise, bright book will prove to be an invaluable aid in understanding the past and the present of a remarkable and thriving country.

Denis Judd
London
2001

CHAPTER ONE

Early Beginnings up to 1760

The first immigrants to an unpopulated North America arrived well over 15,000 years ago. Travelling across a land bridge from Siberia to Alaska, or navigating the waters of the eastern Pacific Ocean, they passed through northwestern Canada on their way south, past and around the glaciers of the last Ice Age. Later they returned from south to north as the glaciers melted, settling around the ice-fed lakes that dotted the centre of the continent.

The Land

Canada has an abundance of geographical extremes. At 3,845,774 square miles it is the second-largest country on earth. It fronts on three oceans — Atlantic, Pacific and Arctic. On Canada's southern border, there are hardwood forests; at its northern extremity, there is perpetual ice, with plant life only a geological memory. The hardwood forests are the exception. Much of Canada is forested, to be sure, but softwood: pine, spruce and other trees that can survive a harsh climate and sparse rainfall make their way between rocks and swamp.

In all, about 3 per cent of Canada's landmass is considered arable (compared to 24 per cent of the United States, or 38 per cent of France). In this, Canada is the product of the Ice Age, the Pleistocene, which saw glaciers advance and retreat four times, covering almost all of the country and penetrating deep into what is now the United States.

The ice left its marks. Circling frigid Hudson Bay, a vast scarp of

Physical map of Canada

0 ——— 500 km
0 ——— 500 miles

RUSSIA

Beaufort Sea

Queen Elizabeth

Banks Island

Melville Island

Victoria Island

60°

Yukon

USA

Mackenzie Mountains

Great Bear Lake

160°

Keele Peak 2972

ROCKY

Mackenzie

Great Slave Lake

Gulf of Alaska

Caribou Mts

Lake Athabasca

PACIFIC

Coast Mountains

Chilco Peak 3049

Peace

Reindeer Lake

Queen Charlotte Islands

M O U N T A I N S

Saskatchewan

Mt Waddington 3994

Fraser

Mt Robson

OCEAN

Vancouver Island

Selkirk Mountains

L. Man

140°W

Missouri

Snake

Over 5000 metres
500-5000 metres
0-500 metres
Glaciers

U

120°

rock, muskeg*, lakes and rivers was scraped by the glaciers, leaving only small pockets of fertile soil. This 'Canadian Shield' occupies between a third and a half of Canada's landmass, creating a northern vision of Canada celebrated by landscape painters and poets. It created, too, a field for exploration and exploitation, from missionary accounts to geological surveys, that define Canada as a gloriously resource-rich territory, a fertile field for investment and development.

This 'Canada of the North' exists, certainly, more visited than inhabited in an urban and developed age. It is familiar to most Canadians, as to the rest of the world, through pictures and tourism. For most Canadians, 95 per cent of them, do not live in the north, but cling to an urban and farming fringe around the coasts and borders of their land, and it is to that fringe of land that settlers have always come.

THE PACIFIC AND THE CORDILLERA

Canada's Pacific coast is part of the western Cordillera that stretches from Alaska to Arizona – jagged ranges of high mountains. The best known are the Rocky Mountains, which lie between 300 and 375 miles inland, but there is also the Coast Range. In between there is the Rocky Mountain Trench, and a rolling interior plateau. The effect of the Coast Range is to dump rain on coastal Canada – as well as to block mild maritime air from penetrating further into the continental landmass. As a result, the interior, between the Coast Range and the Rockies, has low precipitation (as little as ten inches) while the coastline may have up to 80 inches annually. Canada's Pacific Coast also has the country's mildest winters – with daily averages in January hovering at or above the freezing point. From the Rockies to the Pacific, a number of great rivers flow, most importantly the Fraser, whose fertile delta eventually attracted large populations. The east to west direction of these rivers would prove important politically and economically. Today, the Cordilleran region accounts for most of the province of British Columbia, and part of the Yukon Territory to its north.

---

* Muskeg: Cree word for a swamp covered with a thick crust of decomposed vegetation which is common across the Canadian sub-Arctic.

THE GREAT PLAINS

Canada's Great Plains (often, though mistakenly, called the Prairie) stretch from the American border north to the Arctic Ocean, and from the Rocky Mountains east to the Lake of the Woods on the Ontario-Manitoba border. Accounting for 18 per cent of Canada's land area (695,000 square miles) the plains are actually a succession of flat steps, running from east (lowest) to west (highest). The climate of the plains is continental – long, cold winters and short hot summers – though varying in intensity from south to north. Low precipitation is, however, characteristic of the whole region.

The least precipitation falls in the southern parts of the present provinces of Alberta and Saskatchewan; that area comes closest to a true prairie, a flat, treeless sea of grass. Further north, and west and east, there is more rain and more trees – a rolling 'parkland.'

The plains are dominated by two great river systems. The Saskatchewan flows west to east in two branches, rising in the Rockies and flowing into Lake Winnipeg in Manitoba. (The total length of the Saskatchewan is practically 2,500 miles). The Mackenzie River system rises in central and northern Saskatchewan and Alberta and flows 2,634 miles to the Arctic Ocean through or past a series of Western Great Lakes – Athabaska, Great Slave and Great Bear. Both river systems are navigable for shallow draft boats – a point that would prove crucial for Canadian development in the eighteenth and nineteenth centuries.

THE CANADIAN SHIELD

The Canadian Shield's actual extent remains a matter of definition. If it includes the islands of the Arctic, then the shield comprises almost half (46 per cent) of Canada's landmass. If not, then the total is 32 per cent. The shield is a region of rocks and lakes and, as far north as the timber line (beyond which no trees grow), forests. The rocks are among the oldest on earth (Precambrian) and as a result are considerably worn, giving the shield a gently rolling surface. Except for its tree cover, the shield is a barren land above the ground; below, however, it features hoards of minerals, from iron to copper to gold to uranium. North of the tree line, the shield is tundra, with little more than a brief cover of wild flowers and lichen above permanently frozen ground (permafrost).

Not part of the shield, but surrounded by it, are the Hudson Bay Lowlands, formerly the bed of an inland sea, which has now retreated to the present contours of Hudson Bay. Scrub forest dotted by bogs and muskeg is characteristic of this region. Hudson Bay itself – frozen over eight or nine months out of twelve – acts as a kind of vast interior refrigerator, depressing temperatures around it and drawing down Arctic weather into the heart of the continent.

ST LAWRENCE LOWLANDS

The lowlands lie in the Canadian part of the watershed of the St Lawrence and its tributaries – the Great Lakes Basin. Though only 1.8 per cent of the Canadian landmass, it is by far the most densely inhabited, and presumably desirable, part of the country. Canada's best farmland is in this region, an area of moderate winters, much shorter than on the plains, and generally fertile soil. The five inland seas of the Great Lakes (Superior, Michigan, Huron, Erie and Ontario) and their outlet, the St Lawrence, dominate the region, moderating the climate and, in early days, furnishing easy transportation.

APPALACHIAN REGION

The eastern spine of North America is the Appalachian Range, from Georgia in the south to Newfoundland in the north. The Appalachians consist of low-lying mountains, interspersed with lakes and rivers, with occasional pockets of arable land. The Appalachians were the original barrier between European settlement along the Atlantic Coast and the lands of the interior, breached, in the case of Canada, by the St Lawrence River, which permitted ocean-going ships inland as far as Montreal. Though there are some remarkably fertile areas in the Appalachian region, it tends to be more hospitable to forestry and mining than to extensive settlement, at least in its northern, Canadian, end.

First Peoples

The first settlers did not leave their precise date of arrival. Archaeologists studying the remains of Canada's prehistory estimate that human settlement occurred as far back as 20,000 years ago, during the last glaciation. The glaciers covered most of Canada, but omitted some parts of what is now the Yukon Territory in the northwest, and there, at Old Crow, are the remains of an early encampment, approximately 15,000 years old. The Old Crow site appeared to confirm that the settlement of the Americas proceeded from north to south, starting at a land bridge from Siberia to Alaska and moving south down the Cordillera that divides the continent's plains from the Pacific. But that is not the only theory of early human settlement: people may have come by sea as well as by land, skipping the inhospitable and icebound north and landing in the comparatively warmer south.

The glaciers did not finally retreat from the heart of North America until between 14,000 and 7,000 years ago. As they went, people from the south, 'Paleoindians', followed them north, occupying all of southern Canada from Pacific to Atlantic by 10,000 years ago. The climate was notably cooler than today's – what would now be called subarctic – and the coastlines farther out. Glaciers did not finally reach their present dimensions until roughly 7,000 years ago, as the climate warmed to approximately its present temperature.

The Paleoindians lived in small groups, hunted and fished, and carved their tools and weapons from stone – whether on the West Coast, the Great Plains, or the eastern woodlands. Their quarries were the now extinct mammoth and mastodon, as well as the more familiar elk and deer. By 8,000 BC, however, humans on the West Coast had begun to fish rivers for salmon. Eventually, by about 1,000 BC, it is possible to trace village fishing cultures that resemble in many respects those of the West Coast peoples of historic times – an ordered and culturally rich life.

To the east, tools grew more and more sophisticated, from primitive chipped implements to tools of polished stone. Around the upper Great Lakes copper implements appeared, roughly around 3,000 BC, drawing on copper deposits around Lake Superior. Further east, in modern Quebec, while implements were still made of stone, they closely

resembled those of the copper culture, and archaeologists have concluded that waterborne trade, presumably using canoes, existed by
about 2000–1000 BC. Meanwhile the use of pottery spread from west
to east, reaching the Great Lakes region around 1,000 BC.

The boreal woodlands to the north and east of the plains supported
hunting, though in the rich and temperate Great Lakes region hunting
gradually gave way to agriculture, beginning about 1,500 years ago.
Maize, Indian corn, became the staple crop, and with it came a more
settled style of life, in organized villages, moving only as the soil became
exhausted. The mound-building (Adena or Hopewell) cultures,
featuring elaborate burial mounds, spread into modern Ontario;
indeed, one of the largest mound building sites is in north western
Ontario, Manitou Mounds at Rainy River.

THE GREAT LAKES REGION

Sedentary agriculture was still characteristic of the lower Great Lakes
region when the earliest explorers and missionaries arrived there. The
longhouses of the Iroquois peoples dotted the Great Lakes area, and
villages sometimes numbered as many as 2,000 inhabitants. Villages
were made up of a variable number of long houses, arched dwellings
constructed of poles covered with elm bark. The sizes varied: they were
usually about 20 feet wide, but between 50 and 200 feet long. Five to
ten families were grouped in each long house.

The Great Lakes were, in terms of climate, the most favoured part of
Canada, which otherwise did not lend itself to primitive agriculture. In
the Iroquois villages, essentially, men hunted and went to war, while
women were in charge of raising crops, maize (corn), beans and squash,
called the 'three sisters'. Farming was laborious, since apart from the
dog (useless except for companionship and hunting) there were no
domestic animals to take up the burden of heavy farm labour. Activities
varied with the seasons: fishing was best in the spring, and hunting in
the autumn.

THE PLAINS AND EAST COAST

In the northern forests, the Great Plains and along the East Coast, with
a less favourable climate, fishing and hunting were the way of life.

Housing in the Atlantic and boreal forests was wigwams, triangular tentlike structures of poles covered in bark. Woodland peoples fished and hunted, either by trapping or using spears or bows and arrows. On the plains, life turned on the migration of buffalo herds, hunted on foot by bands organized for the purpose of gathering food. Buffalo fed, housed and clothed the people of the plains – meat for food, skins for the coverings of tepees, and men's and women's clothing.

ARCTIC CANADA

Arctic Canada differed. Settlement was later, and the people of the north remain more closely connected to related groups across the Bering Strait in Siberia. 'Paleoeskimos,' ancestors of today's Inuit (formerly called Eskimos) moved from west to east in the Arctic starting about 4,000 years ago, spreading along the northern coast and down the Atlantic seaboard as far as Newfoundland, which they occupied for 1,000 years. Seals, walrus and fish made up the diet and furnished the clothing of the people of the Arctic. It was these early Inuit, called Dorset Culture (after Cape Dorset, where early artifacts were found) who first encountered Europeans.

VIKINGS

Norse adventurers (Vikings) crossed the North Atlantic and settled first Iceland (860 AD) and then Greenland (980 AD). Voyagers from the Greenland colony, under Leif the Lucky, sailed west and south, and later recorded their exploits in stories (sagas). The sagas told of a new place, Vinland, probably meaning 'pasture' rather than 'wine country.' Vinland was only one discovery of several. To the north there was Helluland, a rocky country, probably corresponding to present day Baffin Island. Further south there was Markland, a wooded terrain that is usually assumed to correspond to Labrador. And then there was Vinland, more temperate, suitable for settlement.

Probably between 1002 and 1007 the Norse did settle in North America, but for the next 950 years there was nothing, apart from the traditions of the sagas, to say where. In the uncertainty, liars flourished as Norse 'discoveries' were unearthed from Maryland to Wisconsin. Only in 1960 did the Norwegian archaeologist Helge Ingstad, and his wife Anne, locate authentic Norse traces near the northern tip of Newfoundland, at L'Anse aux Meadows. Excavated between 1961 and 1973, L'Anse aux Meadows yielded traces of three buildings, a few Norse artifacts, and indications of iron smelting. L'Anse aux Meadows was settled sometime between 990 and 1050, tests showed, but only briefly. Nor were the Norse the first inhabitants of the site: the Dorset Culture had also left its mark, and indeed the sagas told of contacts between native inhabitants and the Norse – a tale of death and violence in large part.

The Norse sailed back to Greenland, but did not entirely forget their western landfall. Norse Greenlanders visited Markland for timber as late as the fourteenth century, and contacts were kept up between Greenland itself and Iceland and even distant Norway. But in the fifteenth century all contacts between Greenland and present-day Canada ceased.

Discovery and Early Exploration

The disappearance of the Norse colony did not mean the end of all contact. There were other seafarers in the North Atlantic in the fifteenth century, fishing boats out of England, France and Spain. How far, and how early, these mariners out of Bristol or Brest or Bilbao sailed we cannot know. It was from their experiences, and the legends of the Norse, that Italian captains like Christopher Columbus or John Cabot decided that by sailing west they would reach land – not just any land, but China, or perhaps India. So reasoning, Columbus reached the Bahamas in 1492, and in 1497 Cabot, sailing out of Bristol with the authority of the English king, reached Newfoundland.

Cabot brought with him the claim that the land discovered belonged to Henry VII of England. This fact makes Cabot's voyage not merely the beginning of Canada's written history, but the start of its political history – the origin of English rule. For by discovery came sovereignty, European style, no matter what the original inhabitants of the country might think. For the time being, those inhabitants were almost undisturbed: Cabot's voyage proved, not the possible existence of a western sea highway to India, but the certainty that the ocean off North

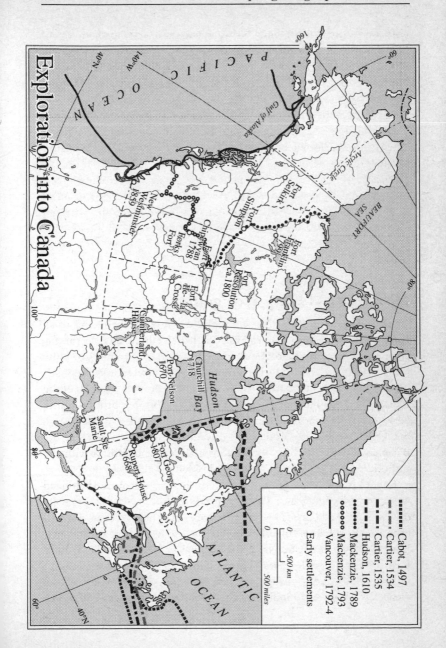

Exploration into Canada

PACIFIC OCEAN

Gulf of Alaska

BEAUFORT SEA

Arctic Circle

ATLANTIC OCEAN

New Westminster, 1859

Fort Selkirk

Fort Simpson

Fort Franklin 1825

Fort Resolution ca. 1800

Chipewyan 1788

Forks Fort

Fort Île-à-la-Crosse

Cumberland House

Fort Nelson

Churchill Bay

Hudson Bay

Sault Ste Marie

Rupert House 1668

Fort George 1807

40°N
140°W
160°
60°
80°
100°
80°
60°
40°N

▪▪▪▪▪▪▪	Cabot, 1497
▪ — ▪ —	Cartier, 1534
▪ ▪ ▪	Cartier, 1535
▬ ▬ ▬	Hudson, 1610
●●●●●●	Mackenzie, 1789
○○○○○○	Mackenzie, 1793
———	Vancouver, 1792–4
○	Early settlements

0   500 km
0   500 miles

America was teeming with fish – thus beginning Canada's history as a storehouse of bountiful natural resources. To Newfoundland came not merely generations but centuries of European fishing fleets until, late in the twentieth century, the fish ran out. The fishing crews sought water on shore, and rest, and a place to dry and cure their fish. Soon some were wintering in Newfoundland, and eventually some stayed for many winters.

The Atlantic fishery was an enterprise of many nations, its fishermen the subjects of many kings: Basques, Bretons, Normans, English, and Portuguese. At first their relations were merely local, but where a subject travelled so did allegiance, and European politics, and eventually war. In one theory, the country first on the ground, with prior discovery, had the best claim; in another, the new lands of the Americas and Asia could be parcelled out by the Pope – as they were, by a Spanish Pope in 1494, between Portugal and Spain.

FRENCH EXPLORERS

Portugal and Spain were too occupied with other, richer discoveries to bother much about the territories across the North Atlantic. Although Portuguese and Spanish explorers brushed the shores of North America, it was left to other countries to try their hand in the regions that Cabot had first sighted. Jacques Cartier, out of St Malo in Brittany, was the next significant explorer of what later became Canada; and it was Cartier who first reported on an Indian name (Algonkian in fact), *kanata,* that meant meeting place. Suitably amended for European tongues, it became Canada.

As usual, this French expedition began in a quest for Asia and, if possible, gold (the riches of Peru had just been found, and the Spanish looting of Mexico was a vivid and attractive memory). Cartier in 1534 sailed past Newfoundland (proving it was an island) and into the great inlet that leads to the St Lawrence River, which he named the Rivière du Canada. (It received its present name early in the 1600s.) Erecting a cross near present-day Gaspé, he claimed and named the land of the St Lawrence for France – New France.

He returned the next year with three ships, passing Gaspé and ascending the St Lawrence River to its first narrows, where he found an

Iroquois village, Stadacona. Cartier then followed the St Lawrence deep into the continent, discovering that it was easily navigable as far as present-day Montreal, then an Iroquois village called Hochelaga. Cartier and his men spent an unhealthy winter at Stadacona, losing 25 of their number to scurvy, and returned to France in the spring of 1536, carrying some of their unwilling hosts with them.

A third even larger expedition followed, although not until 1541, and not under Cartier's command, but under that of the Sieur de Roberval. Cartier, with 1,500 men, left France before Roberval, and once again arrived at Stadacona, where he again spent the winter, this time under siege from the irritated inhabitants. He left for France the next summer, carrying fool's gold and other shiny but worthless minerals. Meeting up with Roberval en route, he ignored the latter's orders to return to Stadacona, and continued on to France. It was the end of Cartier's westward voyaging and the end for the next 60 years of France's attempts to exploit the St Lawrence as the route to India and China. Convulsed by wars between Catholics and Protestants from the 1560s to the 1590s, the French had little time to spend on speculative trips across the Atlantic, and none at all for cold and disappointing Canada.

ENGLISH EXPLORERS

Religion dominated European life and politics in the late sixteenth century. Religious factions fought within countries, and Catholic and Protestant states warred with each other. England, officially Protestant since the accession of Elizabeth I in 1558, feared aggression and subversion from Catholic Spain and waged an unofficial maritime war on the Spanish king's ships and colonies. In pursuit of Spanish gold, Elizabeth's captain Sir Francis Drake sailed around the world in 1577–79, probably sighting Vancouver Island en route. At the other side of the continent, other English sailors sought gold and the Northwest Passage to India, and found instead cold, scurvy and disappointment. Their efforts did add Baffin Island, Frobisher Bay, Davis Strait and the coast of Labrador to the known geography of the world; but it was not an achievement that could be built upon. The Arctic was definitely uninhabitable to all but its native Inuit, given the skills and technology, and the lack of financial resources, of the sixteenth century.

Fishing continued off Newfoundland, and there in 1583 Elizabeth's courtier Sir Humphrey Gilbert founded a short-lived colony, but it mouldered in the foggy climate and then withered from the usual lack of funds. The sixteenth century ended without any permanent establishment from any European power in the Americas, north of the Spanish Caribbean and Mexico.

THE FOUNDING OF NEW FRANCE

The end of the sixteenth century coincided with an abatement of the wars of religion among or within England, France and Spain. The Spanish, repeatedly bankrupt, retired for a time and then refocused their attention and their armies on central Europe and Italy. The French, under a converted Catholic monarch, Henry IV ('Paris is worth a mass,' he quipped), now found time for exploration in the hope, once again, of finding the route to the Indies, the Northwest Passage. A new crew of optimists was sent out to the Americas, under the Sieur de Monts and his navigating lieutenant, Samuel de Champlain, who had earlier travelled up the St. Lawrence, in 1603. They settled on a maritime region first called Arcadia by an Italian explorer in the Spanish service, Verrazano, in 1524: its beautiful trees reminded him of a woodland region in classical Greece of the same name, where nymphs and satyrs frolicked.

Verrazano did not see this American Arcadia in the winter, but de Monts and Champlain did, first on the north shore of the Bay of Fundy, on a small river they named the Sainte Croix. There they spent the winter of 1604–5, abandoning the site as too inhospitable for survival. They moved across the Bay of Fundy to the Minas Basin, much more sheltered, and with far better land, actually suitable for crops as time would show. At Port Royal, as they dubbed their colony, they spent a happier two years, returning to France in 1607. Settlers would return to Arcadia in 1610, this time for good. As time passed they forgot the 'r' in the colony's name: it became Acadia, 'Acadie' in French. Because of the three-year gap in settlement, however, it was not the first permanent French colony in the New World.

Instead, in 1608 de Monts sent Champlain to establish a post at the narrows of the St Lawrence. The term for 'the river narrows' in the local Algonkian language (the Iroquois having retreated southward, and been replaced by another Indian nation) was 'Quebec' (Québec in French) and the term first appears on a map of 1601. Its position at the narrows made Quebec a natural point of entry for ships from Europe, difficult to pass and impossible to ignore. At the same time, smaller vessels, such as canoes, could safely descend the river to Quebec, making it a natural place of exchange between the products of Europe and those of America. New France, as the colony of which Quebec was the centre was named, produced essentially only one thing that Europeans craved – fur. Fashion dictated many uses for fur, for decoration and for warmth, but the glory of fashion, from the seventeenth to the nineteenth century, was the felt hat, made from beaver fur. Beavers flourished in abundance in the interior of North America, and the quest for beavers to supply European hatters proved to be the economic spur needed to draw the French far into the interior of the continent.

NATIVE–EUROPEAN CONTACT AND ITS CONSEQUENCES

The Europeans in exchange for fur offered metal objects – knives, kettles, and muskets – that swiftly displaced the stone and wood tools of the local Indians. They provided cloth, for warmth, and alcohol, for recreation – a dangerous innovation. They brought, though unknowingly, European diseases that overwhelmed Indian immune systems, and that devastated the native populations of the Americas. The aboriginal population of Canada may have numbered as many as one million in 1500; by 1850 it was down to 100,000, and several Indian peoples had disappeared as autonomous societies.

The first of these devastated peoples was a particular favourite of Champlain's, the Hurons, an Iroquoian nation – an alliance of five tribes living in fortified villages and numbering about 25,000 – that lived around the south shore of Georgian Bay, off Lake Huron. There they practised subsistence farming, mostly of corn, hunted and fished. The Hurons were rivals of, and hostile to, the five-nation Iroquois confederacy that lived south of Lake Ontario. They were also experienced traders, and almost immediately took advantage of

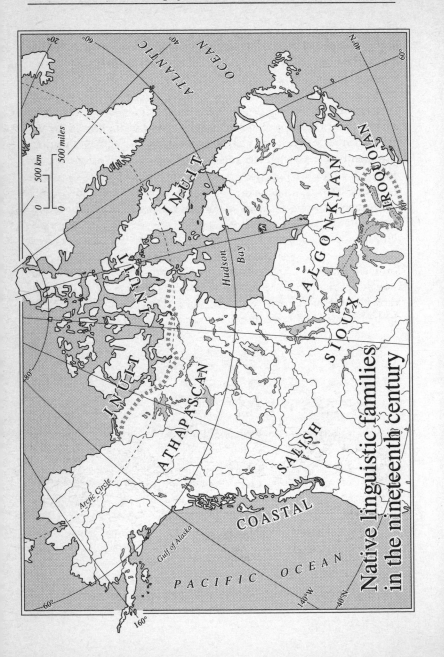

Native linguistic families in the nineteenth century

Champlain's settlement at Quebec to establish contacts. The Hurons hoped to monopolize the French, to the disadvantage of the Iroquois; more, they hoped to ensnare the French in their war against the Iroquois. In both these objects they were successful. French hostilities against the Iroquois began in 1609, a year after the foundation of Quebec. In 1613 and again in 1615 Champlain journeyed to the interior toward the country of the Hurons, wintering there in 1615–16. On the earlier journey, in 1613, Champlain lost one of his navigation instruments, an astrolabe, recovered two centuries later; it now sits on display in a museum in Ottawa, not far from where he lost it.

During his trips, Champlain discovered Lakes Ontario and Huron, and mapped a canoe route up the Ottawa River to Lake Huron that would later become the backbone of the fur trade. And of course he joined the Hurons in expeditions against the Iroquois, who were at first defeated by French musketry. The Hurons seemed to have made a fortunate choice. Champlain did more than bring guns and knives: he brought religion, in the form of missionaries, starting in 1615. The best known of the missionaries were the 'black robes,' the Jesuits, perhaps the best-trained and certainly the best disciplined of Catholic monastic

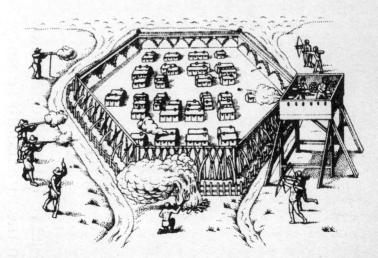

The Hurons and French join in attacking an Iroquois village, 1615

orders at the time. Whether from Champlain and his secular associates or from the missionaries, the Hurons also caught diseases, especially smallpox, that reduced their numbers in the 1630s to about 9,000 – barely a third of the numbers when the French first made contact.

As the Hurons failed, the French settlement at Quebec grew. It was not without its vicissitudes. France went to war with England in 1627, and as a consequence an English fleet appeared before Quebec in 1629, seized the town, and removed Champlain back to England. With the resumption of peace the settlement was returned to France, and to Champlain, who died there in 1635.

Champlain died just as the wars with the Iroquois were heating up. To combat Iroquois raiding parties, the French established a string of posts along the St Lawrence. Of these the most important was established in 1642 at the head of navigation on the St Lawrence; it was called Ville-Marie de Montréal, Montreal in English. Montreal's location was even better than Quebec's, placed as it was where the Ottawa River joined the St Lawrence, in the middle of a fertile alluvial plain, while over the city towered a small volcanic mountain, Mount Royal (more than 650 feet high), from which the city derives its name.

Montreal was intended as a way station en route to Lake Huron, instead it became a beleaguered outpost. Between 1648 and 1652 the Iroquois finally overwhelmed the Hurons, destroying their villages, and killing many of the inhabitants (including missionaries). Not only the Hurons, but all the nations of the Great Lakes region were affected, depopulating what is now southern Ontario and Michigan. The survivors were absorbed by the Iroquois, or fled to the west (eventually ending up in Oklahoma) and to the east, where the largest group formed a mission under the protection of the French, at Loretteville near Quebec, where many of them still live.

The Iroquois wars did not end with the destruction of Huronia, nor were the Hurons the only French allies. The Algonkian peoples who lived in the Northern Great Lakes region saw advantage in an alliance with New France, just as the French sought to replace the vanished Hurons. The Iroquois only temporarily blocked the access of the French to the *pays d'en haut*, the backcountry where the beaver flourished and fortunes could be made. As time passed, New France grew stronger.

THE SLOW GROWTH OF NEW FRANCE

Despite the Iroquois, New France had gradually expanded until by the 1640s it occupied the valley of the St Lawrence between Quebec and Montreal. It did not, however, flourish. Beset by war, it was also starved for funds from home. The funds were supposed to be provided by investors, hoping to make a profit out of the exploitation of the colony, but New France's most reliable product was, instead, debt. Faced with a failing colony, the French government under Henry IV's grandson, Louis XIV, decided in 1663 to assume the administration, and thereafter ran New France as a department of the government in Paris. Instructed by his minister Colbert, Louis sent out 400 troops, sufficient to hold the Iroquois at bay if not altogether defeat them. Next he sent out 850 young women to reinforce the largely male population. With security and fertility assured, New France for the first time had a future.

Society was organized on lines familiar to France. A governor, representing the king, sat on top, in command of the military and charged with the colony's security. An intendant, effectively the treasurer, looked after the economy, including the budget, while a bishop (of Quebec) guarded New France's spiritual health. Settlement was confided to a rank of minor nobility, the *seigneurs*, who opened land, procured and assisted settlers (*habitants* in French), whom they were then entitled to exploit through rents and fees, while retaining enough of their respect to lead them in battle. This eminently logical hierarchical system seldom worked as planned. Governors fought with intendants, bishops clashed with governors, *seigneurs* were ground down by *habitants*.

New France grew, but slowly. The population, 3,215 in 1665, was only 20,000 in 1710, and 55,000 by 1754. These totals compared most unfavourably with other colonial regimes, and especially with the English (later British) colonies scattered along the eastern seaboard of North America. British America as a whole had over 400,000 people by 1710, and 1.5 million by 1755. These were figures that mattered, because between 1689 and 1763 the British and the French went to war four times, 1689–97, 1702–13, 1744–48 and 1756–63. Wars were fought wherever fleets could sail and armies could march, and North

America reproduced, at first in miniature and later on a grand scale, the conflicts of old Europe. Wars meant taxes and supplies, bases that could feed armies and provision ships, and British America had far more of all of these than New France.

Why was New France, relatively speaking, a population failure? France, after all, was much larger than Great Britain in population. All the colonies, British or French, had record birthrates and produced many children. It was not the size of families that made the difference, but the rate of immigration. It was the number of arriving settlers that was deficient, in the case of New France. Except for soldiers, and the single draft of 850 women in the 1660s, the French government did not compel its subjects to leave for the colonies. *La douce France*, with its gentle climate, and its vast fertile lands, did not stimulate an itch to leave. Travellers' and missionaries' accounts of life in New France were not exactly enticing, except for those imbued with a spirit of self-sacrifice: ice and snow in winter, mosquitoes in summer, and massacres and disease in all seasons seemed to be the lot of the colonists. There was no indication that one could improve one's lot across the sea: after all, New France had the same system of governor, intendant and bishop to be found in provincial capitals around old France, enforcing the same laws and the same uniformity of religion as in the old country.

The British colonies, on the other hand, were more attractive. They promised more land and more freedom, and a better climate than New France could ever pretend to. Bankrupts, convicts, religious dissenters, even French and German Protestants fleeing from the fanatically Catholic Louis XIV, found a home in the colonies.

Exploration of the Interior

The French were not entirely without advantages. New France was protected by hundreds of miles of forests, malarial bogs, and mountains that lay between it and the British colonies. The St Lawrence, alone among the rivers flowing into the Atlantic, led far into the continent. French leadership was frequently daring, tactically skilful and strategically adventurous. Explorers showed the way through the Great Lakes. The most daring, Robert Cavalier de la Salle, named his seigneurie, at

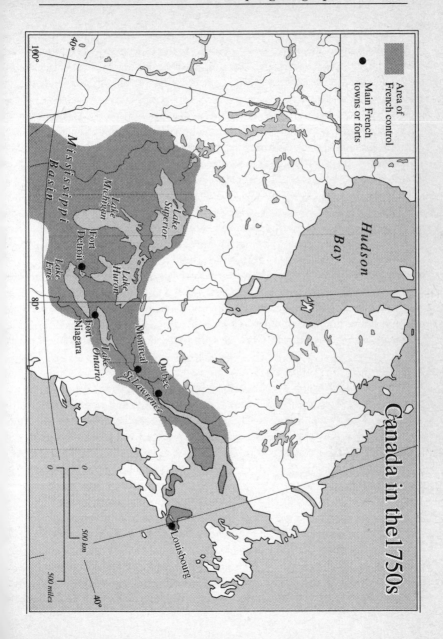

Canada in the 1750s

the rapids on the St Lawrence above Montreal, *La Chine* – China – for he confidently expected to find the route to the Orient and wealth just around the next bend in the river. Instead, he found the Mississippi River, which he traced in 1682 from near the Great Lakes to its mouth on the Gulf of Mexico.

Another Montreal family, the Le Moynes, produced 12 sons, merchants, explorers, soldiers and sailors, who warred against the British from the coasts of Hudson Bay in the north to Havana in the south. One of them, Jean-Baptiste Le Moyne, Sieur de Bienville, went on to found New Orleans in 1718, making the Mississippi a French river.

IMPERIAL RIVALRIES

As the French reached out in the west, their influence shrank in the east. During the War of the Spanish Succession (1702–13) the British used superiority at sea to send a naval expedition against Acadia in 1710 and Quebec in 1711. The British took Port Royal and held on to it in the peace, the Treaty of Utrecht, that ended the war in 1713. The expedition against Quebec, badly led and worse piloted, ended up on the rocks in the St Lawrence. Quebec itself, and New France, thus remained in French hands, while Acadia was ceded to the British.

THE FATE OF ACADIA

But what was Acadia? To the British, it was the mainland of what is today Nova Scotia and New Brunswick. To the French, it was only the peninsula of Nova Scotia, as that area was officially renamed by the British conquerors. Because Nova Scotia was distant and British settlers there virtually nonexistent, the French view prevailed. The French retained the islands in the Gulf of St Lawrence, Cape Breton and Ile St-Jean (today Prince Edward Island), and on Cape Breton they built a great fortress to ward off future British attacks and, they hoped, to undermine the shaky British hold on Nova Scotia and Newfoundland. Louisbourg, named after Louis XV, the child king of France, was one of the most expensive projects ever undertaken by France in the New World.

The stone bastions of Louisbourg, built according to the most advanced military designs, could defend its capacious harbour against attack from the sea. The land was another matter. Louisbourg was surrounded by hills too distant to be enclosed in the town's walls. All that was required was for an enemy to plant artillery on those hills, and pound the walls into rubble, and the fortress must surrender. Successful as a port (the third largest on the Atlantic Coast, after Boston and Philadelphia), and for 20 years a symbol of French determination in North America, Louisbourg fell to British colonial troops almost as soon as the next war broke out, in 1745. Because the British (or rather their American colonists) won this battle but failed to win the war, Louisbourg was handed back to the French when peace was made in 1748. Once again it guarded the eastern gate of New France, as distant New Orleans guarded the south. But in the middle, Anglo-American colonists were overflowing their well-populated colonies in search of land in the wilderness of the Ohio River, where a handful of French troops with Indian allies waited to receive them.

LIFE IN NEW FRANCE

The colony of New France was, in the 1750s, well settled if not exactly well populated. Towns were few: Quebec, the capital, with its mansions for governor, bishop and intendant, a solid bourgeois city made out of stone, in the hope of deterring the fires that regularly razed eighteenth-century towns, was the largest. (Several examples of these houses still exist, though not the palaces of the high officials.) Montreal was second, and it, too, boasted solid houses and mansions built for local notables. (One such, the Château de Ramezay, still stands.) Three Rivers (Trois-Rivières), between Montreal and Quebec, was little more than a village, and beyond that there were six villages – in the whole colony.

Despite official preferences and instructions, most of the *Canadiens*, as the settlers of New France were called, lived in the countryside, in steep-gabled houses made of wood or stone. These were arranged in line along the river, which was the principal, and for many years the only, highway in the colony. (Canadian houses resembled those of Normandy, the province from which most settlers came.) Every so often the steeple of a stone church pierced the sky. Beside the church might be found a school and a few tradesmen's houses, but the farmers lived elsewhere, on their own farms, coming into the settlement only as business or devotion required. Travellers (the few who ever came to New France) found the *habitants* hard working and well dressed – and in the towns more stylish than their British colonial counterparts. Some historians have concluded that the *Canadiens* had become essentially different from the French just over from France, and certainly there were disputes and disagreements aplenty between the locals and their governors. Others, however, point out that such disagreements existed in metropolitan France too, between Paris and the French periphery, and that New France was behaving like other, distant, French provinces.

THE FALL OF NEW FRANCE

Whatever the cause, the last phase of the history of New France was punctuated by dissension between the Canadian-born governor, the Marquis de Vaudreuil, and the French general commanding the army, the Marquis de Montcalm. Quarrelling was not unique to the French. Dissension was no stranger to the other side, where the British had to manage the politics of fourteen colonies from Nova Scotia to Georgia, all of them with elected assemblies and a jealous regard for their rights and liberties, as well as a fixed conviction that the mother country should bear the financial burden of any war with France.

An eighteenth-century French Canadian Soldier

The Seven Years War

The war when it came turned out to be world war, fought in Europe, Asia and the Americas. The war with France in fact broke out in North America. The first clash came in Nova Scotia, where the British governor decided to rid the colony of a French-speaking and Catholic population whose sympathies plainly lay with the French in Louisbourg. In 1755 British and colonial American troops rounded up and deported as many Acadians as they could find, scattering them southward along the Atlantic coastline. Some escaped and some returned, but it is from this dispersion that the Cajun (Acadian) population of Louisiana derives its name. Settlers from Massachusetts took over the abandoned Acadian lands.

1755 also saw clashes in western Pennsylvania and northern New York between defending French and attacking British. All this was without benefit of a formal declaration of war between the French and the British, which finally came in 1756. At first the French were almost uniformly victorious against a British enemy that was divided and badly led. Gradually, however, the weight of British power was brought to bear. The British were better financed, had control of the sea, and were infinitely better supplied. They had local bases in the colonies that could furnish them men and supplies – far more than could the French for their small army in New France.

In 1758 the British attacked and took Louisbourg. This time they demolished its fortifications, which had to await the twentieth century to be restored into a tourist attraction. The same year British forces took Fort Duquesne (renamed Pittsburgh after the British Prime Minister) and Fort Frontenac (modern Kingston, Ontario). The next year it was the turn of Fort Niagara, a stone citadel at the outlet of the Niagara River into Lake Ontario, and Quebec itself.

A very large British fleet – at one point it stretched 60 miles – ascended the St Lawrence River in the summer of 1759 and landed an army opposite Quebec. Stone walls and bastions defended Quebec, like Louisbourg, but unlike Louisbourg geography favoured the defender. The British general, James Wolfe, had first to land his soldiers on the landward side of Quebec's fortifications, but high cliffs and French trenches made this exceedingly difficult. British artillery battered much of the city into ruins, but though this was unpleasant for the defenders, it offered no real threat to their possession of the city. Montcalm, the French general, only had to wait for winter, when the British would be forced to sail away.

Finally, Wolfe spotted a weakness at one end of the French lines, above Quebec City. Under cover of darkness, on the night of 12–13 September his army rowed over to the shore, scaled the cliffs without the French suspecting, and the next morning confronted the French army on the Plains of Abraham west of the city. Superior firepower and better leadership won the day for the British. Montcalm was fatally wounded, while Wolfe was killed outright. Wolfe's death made no difference to the British victory. The French hastily pulled what remained of their army out of Quebec, which surrendered on 18 September.

The war was not over. Montreal was still in French hands, and it was too late in the year for the British to take it. Leaving a garrison in Quebec, the British fleet departed, giving the French a fleeting opportunity to reverse the battle of the Plains of Abraham. The French army tried, besieging Quebec for some months, but in the end failed. Instead, in the summer of 1760 three British armies converged on Montreal, forcing its capitulation on 7 September.

By the terms of the surrender of Montreal, the French army evacuated Canada, taking with it those inhabitants (mainly but not exclusively officials) who chose to go. The English-speaking and Protestant British agreed to tolerate the French language and the Roman Catholic religion, while the inhabitants of the colony were guaranteed, for the time being, their lands and security.

The Treaty of Paris of 1763 that ended the war also ended France's North American empire. The southern part of the empire, Louisiana, centred on New Orleans, was divided between Great Britain and Spain. New France, Cape Breton Island and Ile St-Jean were ceded to Great Britain. France retained only two tiny islands off Newfoundland, St. Pierre and Miquelon as a base for the fishery. The French inhabitants of New France, renamed the 'province of Quebec,' stayed if they wished, and almost all did, keeping their religion, because it was

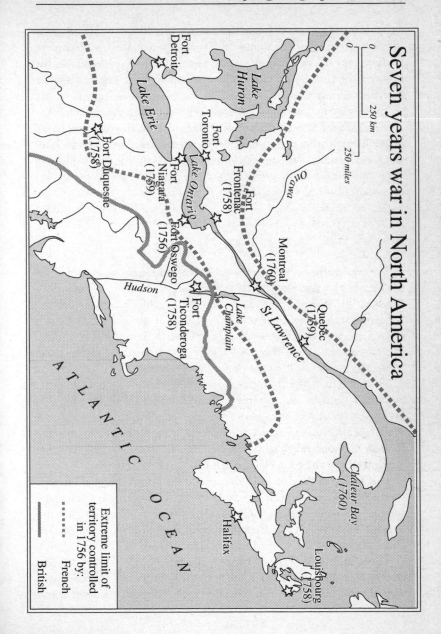

Seven years war in North America

Lake Huron

Fort Detroit

Lake Erie

Fort Toronto

Lake Ontario

Fort Niagara (1759)

Fort Duquesne (1758)

Fort Frontenac (1758)

Fort Oswego (1756)

Ottawa

Montreal (1760)

Quebec (1759)

St Lawrence

Hudson

Fort Ticonderoga (1758)

Lake Champlain

ATLANTIC OCEAN

Halifax

Chaleur Bay (1760)

Louisbourg (1758)

250 km

250 miles

Extreme limit of
territory controlled
in 1756 by:

······ French

——— British

guaranteed, and their language, because no-one could figure out what to do about it.

The news that France was defeated was received rapturously in the British colonies. The French menace disappeared, and the barriers to westward expansion were removed. In the colonies, streets and towns were renamed as variants of 'Wolfe' and 'Pitt.' Only gradually did it sink in that the expansion of the empire had brought two new groups of people under British rule: the French-speaking *Canadiens*, and the Indian nations of the interior. Neither would be easy to deal with, and both would cause problems with the 'old subjects,' the original British Americans from the older colonies.

CHAPTER TWO

An American Revolution,
1760–1820

Until the 1760s Canada shared in the common fate of European settlements in the New World, attached by a colonial bond to Europe, a
fragment of European society in a transatlantic setting. By the 1820s
things were very different. Most of the British colonies in America
achieved independence in the American Revolution. Eventually,
between 1810 and 1825, the Spanish and Portuguese colonies did the
same. Only a few offshore islands in the Caribbean and the Atlantic,
and Canada, remained tied to Europe in a continent that consciously
sought another destiny.

The American Revolution

The fall of Quebec set great events in motion. Twenty years after the
Treaty of Paris ceded the backwoods colony of New France to Great
Britain, another treaty at Versailles confirmed the loss of all but two of
the mainland British colonies in North America. The British were left
with the newest and poorest of their American colonies, Quebec (as
New France had been renamed) and Nova Scotia. What had been the
fringe of a British American empire now became the centre of what
was left of Great Britain in America. Ironically, most of the remaining
British subjects in America spoke French.

Land and money were the occasions for the division between Great
Britain and its colonies. British Americans wanted land, but the Indians
already occupied the available land. The king pledged to protect the
Indian nations, through a royal proclamation in October 1763. The
Indians of the interior chose this moment to revolt, only to be sup-

pressed at great cost. Colonies cost money, the British government reminded itself, and it was only fair that the colonists pay some of their own freight. Yet as the colonists reminded the government, it was equally fair that they consent to their own taxation. Given that the colonies were unrepresented in the British parliament, a constitutional impasse resulted. Tax collectors were tarred and feathered, local officials' homes were sacked and government and subjects girded themselves for a confrontation.

It came in April 1775, in Massachusetts, when the king's troops fired on local insurgents. There followed eight years of civil war, both between Great Britain and America and among Americans themselves. Observers at the time estimated that perhaps one third of the population of the American colonies was loyal to the crown, one third neutral or undecided, and one third revolutionary. It was the revolutionary third, however, that enjoyed the best leadership and the clearest purpose. Early in the struggle, in July 1776, the revolutionary leadership issued a Declaration of Independence, ensuring that there could be no compromise between the colonies and the British government.

The rebels were fortunate in the British generals sent to subdue them. The generals produced victories at first, but time and again they failed to pursue the rebel army and destroy it. Quebec was the exception: separated by hundreds of miles from the rebellion and alienated from a consciously Protestant rebel leadership, Quebec allowed itself to be appeased by British concessions on language and religion. (It helped too that the governor of Quebec, Sir Guy Carleton, possessed genuine administrative and political talent.) When the rebels invaded Quebec, they met a resounding political failure and spectacular military defeat. The rebel commander, Richard Montgomery, perished in a midnight attack on the walls of Quebec City on New Year's Eve, 1775. His army was forced to withdraw, losing as many men to disease as to enemy action. Quebec, and with it Canada, would remain British.

Eventually the rebels formed an alliance with France, which sent an army and enough of a fleet to disrupt British seapower. Isolated and surrounded, the principal British army surrendered to the French and rebel Americans at Yorktown in Virginia in October 1781.

The British were left to salvage what they could. The West Indian colonies and Bermuda were beyond the rebels' reach, protected by the Royal Navy. Nova Scotia, though populated by New Englanders and sympathetic to the rebellion, was isolated by the navy and overawed by a garrison at Halifax, the provincial capital. Hundreds of miles of wilderness separated Quebec from the rebellious colonies, while the St Lawrence allowed the British to keep their garrisons in the Great Lakes supplied. They became reception centres for loyalists fleeing their rebel neighbours, as well as bases for a ferocious guerrilla war along the American frontier.

The peace of 1783 recognized the independence of the United States of America. The treaty established a boundary in the wilderness from the Bay of Fundy on the Atlantic to the head of the Great Lakes in the interior. North of the boundary was what was left of British North America.

British North America in the 1780s

The inhabitants of British North America were of three kinds. The most numerous were the French, the *Canadiens*, numbering about 98,000 in the 1780s. Then there were the Indians, many of whom had fought alongside the British against an American enemy who threatened to dispossess them. And finally there were the British Americans, English-speaking, sometimes loyal, sometimes not. They numbered roughly 60,000 in the 1780s.

The largest group of English-speakers consisted of American refugees. They were of all kinds: Anglican Americans loyal to king and church; Scots immigrants; religious minorities; frontier settlers as well as the urban merchants. Except on the ultimate political question of loyalty to king and country, they differed little from their erstwhile neighbours to the south.

The wounds of the American Revolution were fresh and raw in the first decades after 1783. In many localities the rebels established their authority by terror against the loyalists, who were subjected to various forms of violence, deprived of their property and encouraged to flee. The loyalists, when they could, retaliated in kind.

ANGLO-AMERICAN RIVALRIES

Driven north to Canada, loyalists consoled themselves that the new American republic could not last. It was a point of view that even some American republicans nervously shared. Surely the British would return with their Indian allies: as long as British power remained in America, the American republic would be in danger.

As a result, politics and international relations in the first 40 years of the American republic were dangerously unstable. The generation that made the American Revolution – on both sides – treated its outcome as a stopgap, a piece of unfinished business. British Americans and American Americans were slow to forgive each other, the more so because the differences in the societies they established north and south of the border were slight.

It took some time to work out administrative arrangements for the remnant of British America. Eventually, five colonies were established and given a more or less organized government. Newfoundland, the most remote, was the least organized, under the jurisdiction of a succession of seasonal naval captains who juggled the interests of fishing fleets from Europe and local settler-fishermen. Nova Scotia was divided into three: Nova Scotia proper, centred on Halifax, New Brunswick, with a new capital at Fredericton on the St John River, and Prince Edward Island, formerly the French Isle St-Jean. (There was also, for about 30 years, a separate colony on Cape Breton Island; it was reunited with Nova Scotia in 1820.) New Brunswick, Prince Edward Island and Nova Scotia became collectively known as the Maritime Provinces; Newfoundland, distinct in orientation, government and society, eventually became known as an 'Atlantic' province.

The province of Quebec was divided in two parts, one under-populated and English-speaking, settled mostly by American refugees, one thickly populated and mostly French-speaking. The first, labelled Upper Canada, comprised the fertile peninsula north of the Great Lakes. The second, Lower Canada, consisted of the valley of the St Lawrence.

Except for Newfoundland, the colonies' (or *provinces* as they called themselves) governments were stamped from a single pattern. An

The Upper Canada legislature opened in 1792 by a British official

elected legislative assembly voted revenues to a government headed by an appointed governor sent from Great Britain for the purpose. (Technically the government in all provinces but Lower Canada was headed by a lieutenant governor, while the head of Lower Canada was styled governor in chief.)

It was a typical colonial arrangement, and not all that different from the forms of government enjoyed in the republic to the south, except, of course, that executive authority was appointed from distant London rather than elected by local citizens. The difference from pre-revolutionary days was that London no longer sought to impose taxes directly but begged them from the legislature or made up the difference from funds provided by the British taxpayer and voted by the British Parliament. It was a recipe for an impasse, with resentment guaranteed on both sides. It was a question of who would break first – the colonists who could not control how their taxes were spent, but who could refuse to raise any taxes at all if they wished, or the British taxpayer, who would have to pick up the tab if the colonists would not.

PROSPERITY AND WAR

These clashing fiscal regimes were obscured for a couple of decades because great events abroad took precedence over local affairs in Canada. Shortly after regulating the affairs of British North America in 1791, the British government declared war on revolutionary France in

1793. With brief interruptions, the British Empire remained at war until 1815, at first against the French Revolution and then against the French dictator and self-proclaimed emperor, Napoleon Bonaparte.

The war was a bonanza for the British American colonies. The mainstay of the British war effort was naval power. The navy needed ships, and ships needed timber. The war interrupted supplies of timber from Scandinavia, and so purchasing agents found it in Canada. Rafts of timber descended the water routes of Lower Canada to rendezvous with transport at Quebec City. ('Have you been up to Quebec, donkey-rider, donkey-rider, Piling timbers on a deck? Riding on a donkey . . .' went a sea shanty of the period.) In the Maritimes, and especially New Brunswick, timber was the foundation of a profitable shipbuilding industry, though it did not reach its apogee until the 1840s.

STYLES OF LIFE

As timber flourished, so did Lower Canada. The population doubled every 25 years, and grew from 161,311 in 1790 to 479,288 in 1825. Settlement spread outward from the riverbanks, French-speakers nearer the St Lawrence, English-speakers along the American border where American immigrants took up land grants in a region that came to be known as the Eastern Townships. They brought with them their own system of land measurement too, so that the square surveys of the townships contrasted with the long strip farms of the French-speaking settlements. Architecture in the townships too was American in style, elongated wooden houses that stretched from living quarters back to a summer kitchen in the rear.

The square survey and American-style housing typified Upper Canada as well. The first settlements hugged the shores of Lake Ontario and Lake Erie, linked by schooners in summer and bush trails in winter. New settlements and primitive farming could not sustain much of an economy. Government and government spending on garrisons, forts and supplies provided what subsistence farming and undeveloped trade could not. Fort Malden, Fort Erie, Fort George and Fort Frontenac (later Fort Henry) in Upper Canada, and the elaborate stone citadels in Quebec and Halifax were continually being constructed and reconstructed between 1780 and 1840.

Typical wooden houses of the early settlers

Besides government there was the church – the established Church of England, supported by land grants and government patronage. Anglican churches burgeoned – a bishop and a stone cathedral, built between 1802 and 1804 in Quebec City, another bishop and a wood cathedral in Halifax in 1750, more modest structures elsewhere. In colonies where much of the mercantile elite was Scottish rather than English, worshipping in the established (Presbyterian) Church of Scotland, there were religious rivalries. There were nonconformists, other Protestant sects such as Baptists and Methodists, who vastly outnumbered both Anglicans and Presbyterians. Most numerous of all, thanks to the French Canadians, there were also Catholics, with their own structures and hierarchy, which in Lower Canada dominated public space, marginalizing the officially approved Protestants.

In fact, public life in the colonies was considerably more liberal than in Great Britain itself. Catholics could vote and hold office, while discrimination against dissenting Protestant sects was confined to depriving them of official subsidy. Jews could vote and hold office 50 years before Jewish 'emancipation' occurred in England. And in Upper Canada, almost unnoticed, slavery was gradually abolished starting in 1793, in advance of neighbouring New York or Pennsylvania.

MONTREAL AND THE FUR TRADE

Besides government there was the fur trade. Furs came from the northwest, the country between Hudson Bay and the prairies. Before

1760, the fur trade in this region was run out of Montreal, a fact that attracted English-speaking traders and merchants to that city. The Montreal merchants had a long reach – one of their number, Sir Alexander Mackenzie, discovered a river route to the Arctic Ocean, a river now named after him, in 1789. Mackenzie followed up this triumph in 1793 by reaching the Pacific overland at the mouth of the Bella Coola River, British Columbia.

The Montreal trading interests eventually organized themselves into the North West Company. A system of partners stretched from Montreal into the northwest; some partners were Montreal-based, but most were located up-country, the 'wintering partners' who seldom if ever left the wilderness.

The route from Montreal into the wilderness was long and cumbersome, a thousand miles by canoe from the city to Fort William at the head of Lake Superior, miles more to the prairie at Red River. The birchbark canoes were not the modern recreational variety, but the *canot du maître,* almost 40 feet long, and a crew of six to twelve. They could carry more than two tons of freight. And at Red River there was an alternative route.

The Hudson's Bay Company had long clung to its posts around Hudson Bay. It extended itself slowly and timidly into the interior in the last part of the eighteenth century, using the Hayes, Nelson and Saskatchewan River systems to reach the prairies from its North American headquarters at York Factory. Instead of canoes, the Company favoured 'York Boats' for transport. The York Boat was built on European lines, with a keel, 35 feet long, and two feet deep; it could carry three tons of cargo.

There was a third competitor in the fur trade. The Treaty of Versailles of 1783 set the western boundary of the United States as the Mississippi River. In 1803, by purchase, it acquired the lands between the Mississippi and the Rocky Mountains from Bonaparte's France. American ships cruised around Cape Horn and up the Pacific Coast to the Columbia River, competing with first the North-West Company and then the Hudson's Bay Company.

The War of 1812

The competition was temporarily shelved with the outbreak of war between Great Britain and the United States in June 1812. The war had been impending for some time. The larger war between Britain and France brought in its train a British blockade of the French-controlled continent. The British navy stopped and searched American ships trading with France, and in the process forcibly recruited seamen who might – or might not – have been British subjects. In the west, the American army warred with the Indian nations, who were blocking American settlement south of the Great Lakes. The Indians were in turn encouraged and to some extent supported by the British in Upper Canada. To American sensibilities, it was proof positive that the British still conspired against their independence, and stubbornly refused to treat the United States as an equal. From this sense of grievance, and from the conviction that the Revolutionary War had not solved or settled Anglo-American relations, the War of 1812 came about.

The best solution to British scheming, from the American point of view, was to dispose of the British colonies lingering to the north. Little consideration was given to the French Canadians as a factor, though they were still the largest segment of the colonial population. The English-speaking colonists, however, were ripe for liberation and reunion with their republican cousins.

Issuing a proclamation of republican brotherhood, the American army invaded Upper Canada from Detroit in July 1812. The reaction of the acting lieutenant governor of the province, General Isaac Brock, was initially gloomy. The colony was filled with recent American immigrants, and even the loyalists of the 1780s were at best lukewarm, in his opinion. But the best defence was offence, Brock reasoned, and he moved swiftly to mobilize his small force of British regulars against the invader. He recruited as well the Indian nations of the American northwest – modern Ohio, Michigan and Indiana – under the charismatic war leader, Tecumseh.

Somewhat to his own surprise, Brock was victorious. The American forts of the northwest fell one after the other – Michilimackinac,

The death of the charismatic Indian war leader, Tecumseh, in 1813

Dearborn (Chicago) and Detroit. The American army that had so boldly invaded the province passed into captivity.

It was an unexpected beginning to a war that the Americans believed they could easily win. The republic had 15 times the population of the provinces in 1812. In arable land, manufacturing, income and wealth generally the citizens of the republic far surpassed the provincials. The British were busy in Europe fighting the Americans' unofficial ally, Napoleon Bonaparte, and help from that quarter could come only as an afterthought.

But circumstances were not quite what they seemed. The Americans had a large population, it was true, but it was distant from the theatre of war. The frontier regions up against the colonies were sparsely settled, and communication with the cities of the Atlantic Coast was slow and tedious. The citizenry was not united on the subject of war, or anything else. Bitter partisan rivalry characterized American politics, and mixed with a pronounced sense of regionalism – the republic was, after all, young and its national spirit new and untried – it was a formula for disunity. The New England states barely participated in the war, and in fact they traded vigorously with the colonists before and after the outbreak of hostilities. The British army in Montreal supplied itself from neighbouring Vermont.

As a result the United States was never able to mobilize its full force for a war that many of its citizens refused to take seriously. Using what it had – always too little – the government launched invasion after invasion of Upper Canada, with occasional forays toward Montreal, the colonies' centre of communications. For the first year the British were almost uniformly victorious. General Brock drove an American invading army into the Niagara River in a battle at Queenston Heights in October 1812, though at the cost of his own life. Further west, the British and their Indian allies invaded Ohio, massacring defending American troops.

Around Lake Ontario, a naval race began with British and American dockyards competing to see which could float the most, and biggest, ships soonest. When the Americans had predominance, they could roam the lake, and in April 1813 they used their fleet to capture, sack and burn the Upper Canadian provincial capital, York (now Toronto). A similar war occurred on Lake Erie, on which British communications with Detroit depended. A decisive American victory on Lake Erie in September 1813 forced the British to evacuate Detroit. Retreating, the British and their ally Tecumseh were overtaken and defeated in the Battle of the Thames near modern London, Ontario. Tecumseh perished in the fight.

The Battle of the Thames opened a period of bitter guerrilla war along the Upper Canadian frontier. Some Upper Canadians joined the Americans, and burned out their former neighbours. Their neighbours retaliated by hanging them when they could – 13 in one batch in January 1814 in Burlington. Meanwhile the British crossed the frontier, burning Buffalo, New York and occupying the American Fort Niagara, where they remained for the duration of the war.

Bitter as the land fighting was, it was small scale, and decisive only in that it prevented the Americans from conquering Upper Canada. The war at sea probably had a greater impact on the United States and American opinion. Though the US Navy had some good ships, and some skilful commanders, there were never enough of them, and by the end of 1813 the Americans were swept from the seas. The American coast could now be blockaded, and raided at will.

Using seapower, British and colonial forces occupied eastern Maine in September 1814 and proceeded to administer it for the rest of the war, collecting taxes that were eventually used to found Dalhousie University in Halifax. A British fleet established itself in Chesapeake Bay and levied contributions on the bayside towns. Eventually the fleet landed an army that marched overland and captured Washington in August 1814. The American capital was burned, it was said in retaliation for the burning of York the previous year.

The war lingered on for a few more months, while diplomats laboured at a peace conference in Ghent to bring it to a close. The Americans were happy to settle on the status quo before the war. The British did not care to press for reparations or annexations, and accepted that a war to conquer America would be too costly and too uncertain in its outcome. British and American commissioners signed the Treaty of Ghent on Christmas day, 1814, ending the war.

The Treaty of Ghent did not automatically or immediately create good feeling and mutual respect on both sides of the border. It certainly did not bring the British provinces and the United States any closer together politically. Americans largely forgot the war, and concentrated instead on the expansion into the American west, across the Mississippi instead of across the Great Lakes. It gave a fillip to British American patriotism, compensating, to some degree, for the disasters of the Revolutionary War, of which it was the concluding chapter. The colonists forgot that mostly regular troops and sailors rather than colonial militias won British victories during the war. They had resisted, and they had won. A British American society, provincial, loyal *and American*, would exist beside the republic, contradicting it if not reproaching it. Or so the colonists liked to believe.

The legend of resistance to and successful separation from the United States is half the story – the British half, or what would become the Canadian half of the interpretation of the War of 1812. (There is even a French Canadian variant, turning on the resistance of the Lower Canadian militia to American invasion.)

LIFE WITH THE AMERICANS

There is another side – a tale of continuity and closeness. Society in the provinces – English-speaking society at any rate – continued to resemble life in the states, after 1814 as before 1812. Religion, commerce and legislation were similar and in some cases identical. Governments could limit trade, tax shipping, and build forts and enforce formal allegiances. They could do little to limit the flow of people, ideas, styles and enthusiasms across the border. The distinction between the future Canada and the actual United States was important, as the war had shown. But it was a limited difference that depended on maintaining a North American identity.

CHAPTER THREE

Colonists Become Canadians, 1820–75

In the 60 years between 1815 and 1875, a collection of scattered British colonies along the East Coast of North America became a transcontinental dominion stretching from Atlantic to Pacific and north to the Arctic Ocean. The colonists of 1815, most of them French-speaking, and numbering 430,000 became the Canadians of 1875, numbering four million and mostly English-speaking. Yet Canada remained a British colony embedded in North America, the only sizeable European foothold left in all the Americas. And Canada remained a colony without requiring the presence of a large British garrison and despite its location right beside the United States, a country with more than ten times the Canadian population, and more than ten times Canadians' collective wealth.

It was a result no-one would have predicted in 1815, or in the decades that immediately followed. Canada was, in the 1810s and 1820s, a military frontier of the British Empire. The empire was tightly controlled from its centre, in return for which colonies enjoyed security of trade and military support. The empire supplied colonists, some of them discharged soldiers, the better to defend its borders against Yankees thirsting for revenge for the inconclusive War of 1812.

The Military Frontier

The British government maintained 4,000 soldiers in North America in 1824, scattered from Newfoundland to Upper Canada, plus a major naval base at Halifax, Nova Scotia. These troops had to be housed and defended, and so barracks rose in garrison towns from Halifax to

Windsor, opposite Detroit on what was then the far western frontier. Stone walls encircled Quebec, and an impressive stone citadel dominated the St Lawrence beside the town. Forts, wood or stone, guarded the Great Lakes from Fort Henry near Kingston to Fort Malden in the southwest. Because troops and supplies had to be reliably transported, the British government bypassed the vulnerable St Lawrence River and constructed a series of stone locks along the Ottawa River and the Rideau River, ending in Kingston under the guns of Fort Henry. This Rideau Canal was in its day the single largest public works project undertaken by the British government: it took six years to build (1826 to 1832) and cost £776,000. In today's money this would convert to tens of millions of pounds.

The Rideau Canal was a triumph of technology, as canals were the signature of the advanced engineering skills of the day. Of course, there was no secret to canal building, if the money could be found, and even cheaper and less well-constructed canals served their purpose. The State of New York, at virtually the same time, built its own canal to connect the Hudson and the port of New York with the Great Lakes. Completed in 1825, the Erie Canal had as great an impact on Canada as the rival Rideau Canal route – and perhaps more. For the Erie Canal funnelled immigrants cheaply and reliably from New York to the Great Lakes, filling up the empty lands south *and* north of the lakes. The wilderness barrier between British North America and the United States vanished, a sacrifice to technology, immigration – and opportunity. The United States was no longer just a scattering of blue-coated soldiers and customs agents along the border: the American occupation of the Midwest brought the republic and its republican citizens right up to Canada.

Immigration

The British colonies too were receiving immigrants, and along the same routes as the Americans. Some settlers stopped off in the Maritime Provinces and Newfoundland, but not many. The Atlantic colonies were not large, and unsuitable for large-scale agriculture. New Brunswick, heavily forested, became a centre for sawn lumber and squared timber, and their by-products, shipbuilding and shipping.

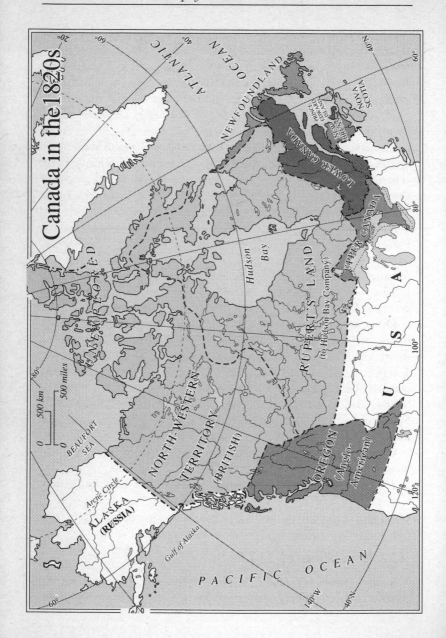

Nova Scotia, almost encircled by the sea, naturally exploited this by fishing and shipping. Newfoundland too grew, both by settlement from the English West Country, and from Ireland. The West Country and Irish speech patterns blended into what is probably the most unusual of Canadian accents, even as the West Countrymen (Protestants) and the Irish (Catholics) battled for decades to see which would be masters of the colony.

The French Canadians of Lower Canada required no reinforcement and in any case received none. The *Canadien* population grew by its own efforts, thanks to a formidable birthrate: partly as a consequence the population of the province rose from approximately 280,000 in 1810 to 670,000 in 1851, and to 848,000 by 1861. Immigration did come to Lower Canada too, English-speaking immigration, some to those parts of the countryside not already settled by *Canadiens* but most of it to the cities, Quebec, Trois Rivières (Three Rivers) and Montreal. Montreal became a majority English-speaking city by the 1840s, and Quebec nearly so. Montreal also became the commercial and industrial centre of Lower Canada, surpassing all other towns in size.

Other immigrants paused briefly in Montreal (or New York City) before moving on to their destination, Upper Canada. This meant a journey by river or canal, expensive and time consuming; but at the end of the journey lay land, fertile and plentiful, and a temperate climate (the vegetation in much of the region is the same as in the South Atlantic states, and the area is called the Carolinian Forest). Settlement in the 1820s and 1830s was steady and the provincial population rose steadily.

Upper Canada was nevertheless at the end of a very long and wearisome journey. Compared to its American neighbours, it was slow and sleepy. Compared to Lower Canada it was underpopulated. Compared to both it was economically backward. The colony needed a jolt, and at the end of the 1830s it received not one but two.

The Rebellions of 1837

The first upset was political. In 1837 discontented colonists rose in rebellion in both Upper Canada and Lower Canada. The origins of the problem lay in the hybrid system of government that Britain imposed on its colonies. Local legislatures, elected by a broad though not universal franchise, had the responsibility of raising taxes; British governors and their appointees had the authority to spend them. It was a system guaranteed to fail, and the miracle was that it lasted as long as it did.

In Lower Canada the situation was complicated, for the first but definitely not the last time, by issues of language, which pitted mostly French-speaking *patriotes* (as they called themselves) against a mostly English-speaking political elite. In Upper Canada the language issue was missing, and the forces for and against the government were evenly balanced. The local lieutenant governor, who had held minor office back in England, even took to the hustings and beat the malcontents at their own game in a provincial election; but the election was a catalyst for polarization rather than appeasement.

In Lower Canada the government had an inestimable advantage: a large force of British troops, to which reinforcements from Upper Canada were added in the fall of 1837, as rebellion appeared certain. Fortunately for the government, the rebellion was not widespread, and the army commander, who had served with Wellington at Waterloo, was both decisive and ruthless. Marching around the countryside, he beat the rebels in several small skirmishes, and terrorized the countryside. The rebel leaders fled to the United States, leaving their unfortunate followers liable to hanging or transportation to Australia, then a penal colony.

The rebellion took a slightly different course in Upper Canada, but the outcome was the same. Lacking troops, the authorities raised the local militia. The rebels marched on the provincial capital, Toronto, where their leader, William Lyon Mackenzie, an excitable and diminutive Scot, had once been mayor. Amateur soldiers commanded by the sheriff put them to flight, and Mackenzie fled for the border, poverty and obscurity.

The rebels' aim had been independence, and a republican form of government. The rebellions took place next to the United States, which regarded itself as the beacon of republicanism and resistance to tyranny. A successful rebellion would almost certainly lead to annexation to the United States, and the Americans were not shy about appropriating territory. Why, then, did not the Americans intervene?

The answer is two fold. First, the United States government did not want to intervene. It took little interest in the British colonies, did not regard them as a threat, and preferred to concentrate its attentions at home. The American authorities accordingly sent a general, not to invade British territory, but to enforce American neutrality. Here the second factor comes into play. While there were private American sympathizers with the republican rebels, they were a minority, even along the border. Had the British been less successful in suppressing the rebellion, sympathy in the United States for the rebel cause might have grown, but as things stood in 1837–38 the insurgents were a lost cause. A few minor incidents occurred in 1838, the colonial authorities hanged a few more rebels, and the rebellion was over.

Reform

The rebellions, though unsuccessful, shook the British colonial structure. The government in London sent out a commissioner (who doubled as governor general), Lord Durham. Durham traversed the colonies, consulted, observed, and returned to Britain, where he wrote a report recommending sweeping changes in the way the North American colonies were governed. In Upper Canada he found power concentrated in the hands of 'a petty, corrupt, insolent Tory clique,' – Durham was a Liberal – and urged instead that government be based on the majority in the legislature. This would, he hoped, make for both more responsible and more effective government.

Language complicated the solution for Lower Canada. There, Durham claimed he had found 'two nations warring in the bosom of a single state.' To solve this problem, he recommended disestablishing the French language (guaranteed by the old Quebec Act in 1774), assimilating French speakers, and in the meantime making them a political if not demographic minority by joining Upper Canada with Lower Canada. In the resulting 'big' province of Canada, Lower Canada, though more populous, would have the same number of representatives in the united legislature as would Upper Canada.

It was an elegant scheme and some observers right up to the present have found Durham's logic persuasive. But politics, which Durham enabled for the first time, produced a different result. Imitating (and inspired by) the British party system, political grouplets emerged, at first regional but later comprehensive. Upper Canadian English-speaking Conservatives found allies in French-speaking Lower Canada. When a French Canadian political leader found himself defeated at home, his English-speaking colleagues found him a seat in the heart of English-speaking Upper Canada. Soon, all politicians agreed that Durham's diagnosis of linguistic war was too pessimistic, and that cooperation among language groups was not only desirable but essential.

Durham had also hoped to reserve the direction of the government to the governors sent out from Britain. The only way this could be managed was to turn the lieutenant governor or governor general into a party leader and have him lead his party in elections. The alternative was to turn the office of governor into a ceremonial and representational function. For all local purposes, the governor would serve as the Queen's representative, acting according to the wishes of whatever majority elections threw into the local legislature. Party leaders would become heads of government, chairing cabinets chosen from among elected party supporters in the legislature. Only foreign relations and defence were in effect reserved. Otherwise, the colonials would get the government they wanted, and wished to pay for.

The Transportation Revolution

This political revolution was accompanied by a technological one. The eighteenth century was the age of sail and waterpower, employing technologies that were old before the Romans. The nineteenth century was the age of steam and of the telegraph. Steamboats came first (the first one to ply Canadian waters, the *Accommodation*, dated from 1809). Transportation time was cut drastically, at least during the months when ice did not cover the waters. Steam for industry came in more gradually, because Canada did not have a great deal of industry. Yet by the mid-nineteenth century steam-powered sawmills, steam-powered textile factories and other industrial establishments were a

The first steamer of the year arrives in Montreal in April 1814

commonplace across the colonies. Finally there was the railway. The governor general in 1837 inaugurated the first railway in Canada, a few months before the rebellion. Next came railways to the United States, to the Atlantic ports that operated the year around, unlike frozen Quebec and Montreal. Railways could not do everything, or do everything cheaply. For heavy traffic there were canals along the St Lawrence and between Lakes Erie and Ontario, all constructed even as late as the 1840s. But canals and railways had one thing in common: they were both subsidized, and subsidized heavily, by the taxpayer.

Revolution in Trade

Along the canals and over the railways came immigrants and imports. They were made for exports too, and their builders assumed that the export trade would help repay their heavy costs. Under the British imperial system, Canadian grain (corn in British English) had a sure market in Great Britain – as did American grain if shipped through Canada. It was a promise as immovable, as solid, as the British Empire itself. In Montreal, Canada's great port, prosperity, actual or anticipated, caused old stone houses to be torn down, and replaced by new warehouses of brick or stone. The city spread up the hill, toward Mount Royal, and its new suburbs were topped off by the elegant mansions of the merchants.

Unfortunately for their hopes the empire twitched. The doctrine of free trade was sweeping through British politics. The Prime Minister, Sir Robert Peel, adopted free trade as a policy, and repealed the preference colonial grain had enjoyed in the British market in 1846. The news caused great indignation among colonial merchants, and particularly in Montreal.

Montreal at the time was serving as capital of the Province of Canada, which meant that the governor general, Lord Elgin, could hear Montrealers' indignation directly. Already enraged by a proposal that would compensate property owners who had suffered during the rebellion of 1837 (compensation for all losses, and not just those of the victors), an English-speaking mob stoned the governor's carriage and burned down the provincial legislature. Next, prominent merchants signed a manifesto calling for the annexation of Canada to the United States.

The storm quickly passed. The capital was moved for safety, to alternate between Toronto and Montreal. Government functionaries could travel up and down the new rail line that by 1860 stretched from Sarnia, at the outlet of Lake Huron, all the way to Rivière du Loup on the St Lawrence below Quebec. This railway, the Grand Trunk, was a feat of engineering – some of it spectacularly good, like the Victoria

The English-speaking mob burns down the Canadian legislature in Montreal in 1849

Bridge (almost 3,000 yards long) that spanned the St Lawrence at Montreal and which is still in service; and some of inferior quality as desperate contractors strove to complete the roadbed within their means. Some observers claim that rail travellers in central Canada can still feel the jolting effects. The Grand Trunk was also a monument to British investment, which poured into Canada, as into the United States, during this period.

The termination of the British protective tariff system did more than frustrate Montreal merchants, or give British consumers cheaper food. It was the death knell for British regulation of Canadian commercial policy. Colonial politicians already controlled local taxes; now they were free to dabble in tariffs as well.

Lord Elgin, governor general from 1847 to 1854, exploited the situation. Canadians, even English Montrealers, needed free, or at any rate freer, trade, he reasoned. Given that incentive to prosperity, their political complaints would vanish like the hot air he shrewdly judged them to be. The solution, as he saw it, was to shore up British loyalty with American trade. Would the United States oblige?

RECIPROCITY WITH THE UNITED STATES

Visiting Washington in 1854, Elgin found American politicians ready, for a variety of reasons, to cooperate. The great issue in the United States was slavery, and the consequent division between Southern slave states and the increasingly militant free states of the North. Southerners, Elgin found, wanted Canadian goods – especially fish from the Maritime Provinces. Northerners, on the other hand, competed with Canadian natural products but were attracted by the notion that increased trade with Canada might bring the provinces into the republic, as free states of course. Elgin augmented his arguments with a grand style of hospitality that greatly helped the Canadian cause.

The result was what would now be called a sectoral free trade agreement. It removed duties on Canadian (and American) agricultural, fishing, mining and forest products, while maintaining them on manufactured goods. Many American politicians hoped that it would assist Canada into the Union, while Elgin assumed that it would do precisely the opposite.

Elgin proved the better prophet. Canadians took full advantage of the opportunity to export their goods to the United States. Trade was actually enhanced when, in 1861, civil war broke out between north and south. Americans clamoured for Canadian goods and got them. Some Canadians, perhaps as many as 50,000, served in the US Army, whether for principle or profit (a few were kidnapped by profit-hungry recruiters).

Canadians divided their sympathies during the American Civil War. Many, probably most, abominated slavery and applauded the Northern cause insofar as it was aimed at slavery's abolition. At the same time, many, and probably most, found American ('Yankee') presumption deplorable, and took quiet satisfaction in some of the Northern defeats, while hoping nevertheless for an end to the slave system.

Great Britain was 'nonbelligerent' – neutral up to a point, but not entirely indifferent to Southern blandishments. British North America was nonbelligerent too, which did not prevent Southern sympathizers from taking up residence in Toronto or Montreal or Halifax, occasionally raiding into Northern territory. On one occasion, in 1864, a Canadian judge actually freed Southern guerrillas, who had invaded Vermont and robbed a bank, and allowed them to keep their loot. Northerners were not pleased.

The North was irritated as well by Canadian tariffs that rose higher and higher on manufactured goods. Plainly political union with the provinces was not about to occur simply because of the blessings of free trade with a cooperative America. In March 1865 the United States government gave notice that it would terminate the Reciprocity Treaty in a year's time. If the carrot would not work on the stubborn colonists, why not the stick? What would the colonies do now? What could they do?

Regionalism and Unity

British North America in the early 1860s was little more than a geographical notion. It did not even have a common political structure. True, Queen Victoria and her ministers in London claimed sovereignty over the lands north of the United States, even though their exact extent was still a matter of speculation. Some of British North America's inhabitants – the aboriginals of the Great Plains and the Arctic – had no idea that there was such a person as Queen Victoria or such a thing as the British Empire. The territory of the Hudson's Bay Company, Rupert's Land, covering more than half of present-day Canada, barely had an administration, certainly not enough to qualify as a colony. British Columbia, prior to a gold rush in the 1850s, had hardly any white inhabitants outside fur-trading posts. Its territory was only organized as a colony in 1858.

On the Atlantic Coast, Newfoundland, scantily populated along the coast and completely uninhabited in its interior, had eventually achieved responsible government but still required occasional interventions by British troops to keep order among a populace divided along occupational, religious and geographical lines. The Maritime Provinces, New Brunswick, Nova Scotia and Prince Edward Island, had more people and more money: the 1850s and early 1860s would long be remembered as a period of prosperity. But it was prosperity based largely on trade, and bad relations with the United States, as well as the prospective cancellation of the Reciprocity Treaty, caused deep unease.

The Province of Canada was the largest and most prosperous of the North American colonies. Its problem was politics rather than economics, and at the root of its politics was a problem in demography. The assumption behind the forced union of Upper Canada and Lower Canada in 1840 was an equality of seats between Upper and Lower Canada. The growth of a vigorous party system negated the anticipated benefits of that equality (English predominance); even more, the growth of the population of Upper Canada undermined the fictional but (from an Upper Canadian point of view) acceptable political equality.

Starting in the 1850s, reformers in Upper Canada (the forerunners of the Liberal Party) demanded an adjustment in the number of seats. Lower Canadians, especially French speakers, naturally resisted. The result was deadlock. An Upper Canadian majority and a Lower Canadian minority (Liberal) balanced a Lower Canadian majority and an Upper Canadian minority (Conservative). Governments rose and fell on the basis of a handful of votes in the legislature. Controversial legislation could not be passed. At a time of tension with the United States, the government of Canada could not pass legislation to provide for defence, much to the disgust of the British government, which paid most of the resulting defence tab. If the Canadians would not pay to defend themselves, British politicians pointedly asked, why should the British taxpayer shoulder the burden?

It was a good question. It was all the more pertinent because British military advisers concluded that Canada was, in fact, indefensible. The Maritime Provinces, because they were more remote, had a slightly better chance, but even there the odds were not too favourable. The United States in the 1850s had passed Great Britain in population. American railways ran directly to the border, and millions of Americans lived within an easy march to Canada.

Nor were colonial links to the mother country especially strong. Canadian governments since the passage of free trade in Britain levied tariffs freely on British goods, and the British government could, or would, do nothing about it. Sentiment and pride were important considerations, especially because British North Americans remained vociferously loyal to empire and crown, and it was difficult for any British government to throw professed patriots overboard. The temptation was, nevertheless, there.

Desperate circumstances sometimes call forth unexpected strengths. Paradoxically, colonial politics, notoriously provincial in outlook and self-seeking in practice, produced a number of leaders capable of drawing conclusions from the signs around them. John A. Macdonald and George Brown in Upper Canada, who were political opponents, and George-Etienne Cartier in Lower Canada, Leonard Tilley in New Brunswick and Charles Tupper in Nova Scotia, decided to risk their futures on a larger stage.

In a series of conferences between 1864 and 1866 these colonial politicians and their allies decided to create a federal union, similar to the United States in most respects, but linked still to the British Empire. Loyal subjects of the Queen, they hoped to call it the Kingdom of Canada, but on British advice renamed it the Dominion of Canada, as less likely to offend republican sensibilities south of the border. In other

Sir John A. Macdonald, the first Prime Minister of the Dominion

ways the British government was fully cooperative, welcoming federation of the colonies and using its remaining (and quite substantial)
influence to overcome opposition in New Brunswick and Nova Scotia.
A British North America Act federating the colonies was drafted and
passed through the British Parliament in March 1867, effective the
following July 1.

THE CANADIAN CONSTITUTION

The new Dominion was a colony still, but in internal self-government
its authority was virtually complete. Foreign affairs remained the province of the British government, but taxes, tariffs and even defence
would be handled locally. A governor general continued to represent
the British government and still had substantial influence over local
affairs, not to mention glamour and prestige in a limited colonial
society. Actual government, however, lay in the hands of a Canadian
federal Parliament, composed of an elected House of Commons and an
appointed Senate. Cabinets, headed by a prime minister, were selected
from among the majority in the House of Commons, on the British
model. If a government were defeated on a vote of confidence in the
House, it would resign or call an election, also on the British model.

The politicians of 1867 imitated Great Britain in their parliamentary
institutions, but they drew lessons from the United States in their

design of a federation. The American federation that they knew had recently fallen apart in a ferocious Civil War. This was attributed to an insufficiently powerful national government, and so the Canadian variant was given more power, more explicitly than the American model. The provinces – Nova Scotia, New Brunswick, Quebec and Ontario, the latter two recreated out of former Lower Canada and Upper Canada – were to manage local affairs, with limited powers of taxation.

What was unusual about the Canadian constitution was its attention to the questions of language and religion. Religion was not disestablished, as in the United States, but given explicit control over schools in Quebec and to some degree in the other provinces as well. 'Separate' (meaning Catholic) schools sprang up in Ontario, while 'Protestant' schools were established in Quebec. French was permitted in the Dominion parliament and courts, and in the Quebec legislature and courts.

THE CANADIAN POLITICAL SYSTEM

The party system gave these institutions their breath of life. The nineteenth century was a partisan age all over the western world, in Britain, the United States and, naturally, Canada. In Canada, two national parties existed, virtually from the beginning: Conservatives and Liberals. Parties governed according to a spoils system that rewarded their supporters with jobs and contracts, and punished their opponents. Partisan newspapers enlivened debate with their ferocious and unbalanced accounts of public life. The first prime minister of the Dominion, the newly knighted Sir John A. Macdonald, was either a brilliant Conservative statesman or a hopeless, unprincipled, Tory drunk, according to taste (there was convincing evidence for both views). His lifelong opponent, George Brown, the Liberal leader, was either a local patriot devoted to economic progress and political equality, or a desperate Protestant bigot. Again, there was evidence to support either case – or both.

What was remarkable was how the secular religion of politics brought together the disparate parts of the new country of Canada, and provided a stable vehicle for government among people who pre-

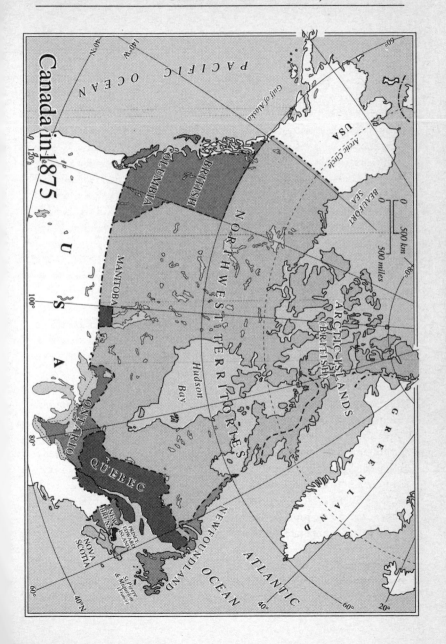

Canada in 1875

viously had little to do with each other. The 1867 political arrangement was sufficiently inclusive to be attractive, and, as it proved, stable. Yet not everyone or every place was included, and dealing with the omissions of 1867 proved difficult.

KEEPING THE EAST

Union with Canada was a sickly growth in the east. Only two out of four Atlantic colonies had joined Confederation in 1867, Nova Scotia and New Brunswick, and in those two it was doubtful if a democratic majority for joining existed. Canada rested on two pillars, as far as New Brunswick and Nova Scotia were concerned. One was the absence of any clear alternative; the other was British determination to see the merger through. The British government was deaf to Maritime pleas for release from Canada, while Maritime voters did not wish to consider the possibility of union with the United States.

With no way out, Maritimers gradually and grudgingly began to explore what Canada had to offer. Sir John A. Macdonald rose to the occasion, doling out offices to his erstwhile opponents while conciliating public opinion with public works and an Intercolonial Railway that eventually reached Halifax in 1877. Anti-Canadian sentiment was left leaderless, and without focus.

There remained the question of the two missing provinces, Prince Edward Island and Newfoundland. Both attracted a certain amount of attention from the United States because both had easy access to the offshore fishery. That was something the Americans wanted, and the Canadians were determined to deny them. American interest guaranteed Canadian attention, especially where Prince Edward Island, located deep in the Gulf of St Lawrence, was concerned. Prince Edward Island brought two items to the bargaining table with Canada: its location, which the Canadians coveted, and its debts, which they were prepared to pay for. A bargain was struck, and Prince Edward Island joined Canada in 1873.

Newfoundland was another matter. More distant, facing out into the Atlantic and east toward Europe, Newfoundlanders saw no good reason to join Canada. Fish was their link to the outside world, supplying the West Indies, or Portugal and the rest of Western Europe.

The Newfoundland elite had no desire to be supplanted by Canadian carpetbaggers, while the island's contending religious adherents could not agree on whether joining Canada was a good thing or a bad thing. And so Newfoundland was left to its own devices and thus it continued for the next 80 years. Canadians accepted the situation with equanimity: by the time negotiations with Newfoundland finally collapsed, in 1869, their attention was fixed elsewhere.

SECURING THE WEST

The prairie west caught Canadian attention long before there was a Canada. The west offered opportunity, escape, and prosperity. Absorbing the west, Canadian visionaries believed that their country could achieve a population in the tens of millions, rivalling the United States. All that would be required was to nudge the Hudson's Bay Company out of the way and appropriate millions of acres of farmland for land-hungry Canadian farmers. With Confederation achieved, the Canadian government set about implementing this vision.

At first everything went smoothly. All the Hudson's Bay Company wanted was money and commercial opportunity. In return for money and land – $1.2 million (a huge sum in 1869) and 5 per cent of the total arable land — the Company surrendered Rupert's Land, its western domain. The British government guaranteed a loan to the Canadians, and the transfer of Rupert's Land was set for December 1, 1869. Sir John A. Macdonald appointed a lieutenant governor for the new territory, and the governor set off for his new post, using the most convenient route, through the United States. But when he reached the border of Rupert's Land, he found his way blocked. The local inhabitants, it appeared, objected.

THE FIRST RIEL REBELLION

Trouble could have been predicted. There was one substantial settlement in Rupert's Land, clustered around the Hudson's Bay Company's post at Fort Garry, in the fertile Red River valley. A population of whites and Métis (people of mixed white and Indian ancestry, and speaking either French or English) traded, hunted and farmed in that area, with only the feeble hand of the Company to administer them. The advent of a new, unknown but almost certainly more effective government alarmed many in Red River, who feared for the security of their lands and their livelihood under a new set of laws. A bitter dispute followed between Canadian immigrants to Red River and the dissidents, but the latter were better armed and better led.

A leader of talent emerged among the Métis – Louis Riel. Young (26 in 1870), well educated and with a gift for political leadership, Riel proclaimed a 'provisional government' whose mission was to negotiate for better terms with the government of Canada. Baffled by the situation, Macdonald did two things: he refused to take ownership of Rupert's Land, and he appealed to the British for help.

Help took the form of a British and Canadian military force. That force would have to come from central Canada and cross 1,000 miles of lakes, rocks, and forests. Until it could reach Red River, Macdonald temporized and Riel negotiated. So far so good, except in the eyes of the pro-Canadian party in Red River, which made its dissatisfaction loudly known. Riel arrested one of the Canadians, a man of doubtful temperament named Thomas Scott, and had him tried and shot for sedition.

It was an unlucky and, for Riel, disastrous act. His provisional government was not a legal body, and it went without saying that it had no legal basis to put anyone to death. Scott's death thus became murder in the eyes of Canadian authorities and aroused public opinion in Scott's home province of Ontario. Riel's hasty and foolish action meant that as the Anglo-Canadian army approached Red River in August 1870 he was forced to flee over the border to the United States.

Riel's fate did not greatly influence events back in Red River or, as it now became, Canada. Macdonald agreed to create a new postage-stamp province, Manitoba, out of the Red River settlement. Existing land titles were guaranteed, and further land was set aside for the children of Métis families. French as well as English became an official language in Manitoba, which seemed to promise a bilingual future for the prairies. Federal money kept the province afloat until it could generate enough revenue to maintain itself.

THE INDIANS OF THE NORTHWEST

The Indians of the northwest had also not been consulted about the acquisition of their homeland by Canada; nor would they be. The Canadian government intended to apply to the Indians of the west the system that had been applied to the natives of central Canada: cession of land by treaty to the government, with natives thereafter restricted to government-run reserves. In the meantime, the government organized and sent west a police force, the North-West Mounted Police (NWMP), the ancestors of the future Royal Canadian Mounted Police (RCMP).

Had the government acted as trustee for the natives it intended to displace, the police might have been sufficient. But the government would prove to be an improvident and irresponsible steward, and as a result, very soon, the police would not be enough. But for the moment the government focused on another, more distant vision: extending Canada to the Pacific.

THE WESTERNMOST PROVINCE

Great Britain's Pacific province had only just been organized when Canada came into existence. Originally two colonies, British Columbia (the mainland, originally called New Caledonia until the British government learned the French had a colony of the same name) and Vancouver Island, the province was merged at the behest of the British government and through the instrumentality of Governor Frederick Seymour. The combined legislature of the new province of British Columbia then moved the capital to Victoria at the south end of Vancouver Island. (Seymour, who was addicted to 'cocktails all day,' soon after expired of alcoholism.)

British Columbia's prospects were poor. A population of 12,000 sat uneasily atop 366,000 square miles of forest and impassable mountains. Like the colonists to the east, British Columbians rejected union with the United States as inconceivable. A link with Canada seemed the only hope, and Canada was willing to bargain. In return for a promise that the Canadian government would build a transcontinental railway, British Columbia joined Canada in 1871.

The majority of the province's inhabitants, the Indians, were not consulted. By the 1870s, the Indians of the Northwest Coast had been in contact with whites for a century, and the impact of the fur trade and of missionaries was considerable. European diseases to which the Indians had no natural resistance ravaged the villages along the coast, while the easy availability of European- or American-made goods undermined the traditional economic structure of Indian societies. Demoralized and weakened, Indian bands increasingly gathered around trading posts, in many cases to practice new lifestyles under the stern direction of missionaries convinced that earlier, heathen ways were deplorable. Under Governor Douglas (1856-64) the Indians were gathered into reserves scattered around the colony, and the Canadian government, which had jurisdiction over Indians, inherited the system, such as it was, in 1871.

The Fall of the Macdonald Government

The acquisition of Prince Edward Island and British Columbia filled out most of Canada's dimensions from 'sea to sea', the motto chosen for the new dominion on its coat of arms. As an afterthought, the British government turned over jurisdiction over the Arctic archipelago, much of it still unexplored and most of it uninhabited, to Canada in 1880.

The Macdonald government did its best to consolidate its domain. The first priority was railways, from central Canada to Halifax in the east (completed in 1877) and to the Pacific Coast. To build the Pacific railway, Macdonald followed American practice and enticed a group of investors with offers of land and subsidy; in return the would-be railway barons subsidized Macdonald and his Conservative Party, which was facing a stiff fight in the second federal election of 1872. The bargain became public after the election, and the result was the defeat in Parliament of the Macdonald government in the fall of 1873.

The ramshackle Liberal Party (cobbled together from groups whose sole common interest was that they opposed Macdonald) was the beneficiary of the 'Pacific Scandal.' The Liberals won a general

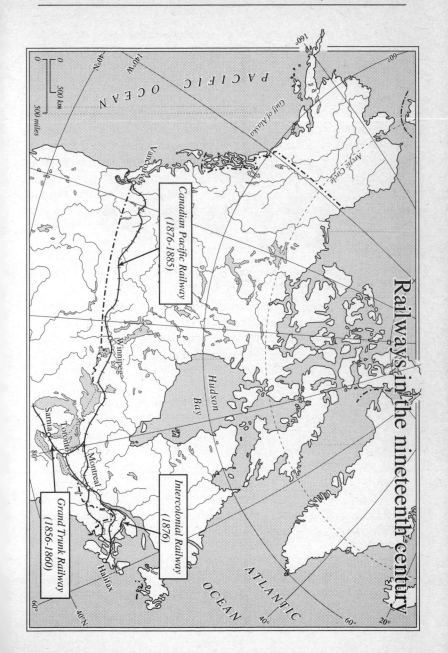

Railways in the nineteenth century

Canadian Pacific Railway (1876–1885)

Intercolonial Railway (1876)

Grand Trunk Railway (1856–1860)

election (Canada's third) in 1874 and entered government just as Canada, like most of the western world, entered a prolonged economic downturn.

The promise of Canada, it seemed, would have to be postponed.

CHAPTER FOUR

Late Victorian Canada,
1875–1919

'The prospects of Canada are truly great!' a late nineteenth-century promoter proclaimed to the world. To which many Canadians of the day might have sourly replied, 'But only in the future.' As the nineteenth century drew to its close, Canada appeared to be a land of eternal tomorrows, a bright future lurking behind a receding horizon. Vast, richly endowed, but cold, remote and inaccessible, Canada's prospects paled beside those of the United States and Australia and Argentina. Many Canadians recognized the fact by moving: Canadian-born residents of the United States totalled 16 per cent of Canada's population in 1910.

In the late 1890s, conditions at last improved. Rising prices for raw materials, falling costs of shipping, the closing of the American frontier, meant better times for Canada. Emigration plunged and immigration soared. The Canadian plains filled up, while the mining industries of Ontario, Quebec and British Columbia boomed. The Canadian government was so optimistic that it sponsored two new transcontinental railways. Only later would the bill be presented and by then, Canada was overwhelmed by external events. Canadians in the late nineteenth century clung to the British Empire, even though their style of life, their culture and their accents closely resembled those of the adjacent United States. Canadian troops served in the South African War (1899–1902) and when the call of duty came in August 1914, when Great Britain declared war on Germany and World War I broke out, Canada was automatically and enthusiastically involved.

World War I – known to contemporaries as the Great War – affected virtually every part of Canadian society. Canada sent an expeditionary force to Europe, to serve in the British army on the Western Front. Canadian industry strained to produce armaments while Canadian farmers harvested bumper crops for Britain. Later the achievement would be remembered with pride; at the time it produced inflation, labour strife and division between English and French Canadians. The slaughter in the trenches of France and Belgium cast doubt on the management of the war, combined with the respectable performance of the Canadian army in France, made Canadians less awestruck by empire, and more confident of their own achievements. When the war ground to an end in November1918 it was a much-altered Canada that faced its aftermath. With war's end, Victorian Canada may also be said to have ended.

Depression and Discontent

Bad economic times dominated public life in Canada in the 1870s and 1880s. The economic downturn of 1873 bore bitter fruit in visible unemployment (though no-one could say how severe) and emigration (though until the census was taken in 1881 no-one could say how much). For the urban unemployed, there was local relief – charity from churches and grudging aid from local governments. The prevailing view was that unemployment, or want and destitution of any kind, was a sign of improvidence and moral weakness, to be succoured, of course, but also to be discouraged.

The solution was more farms in the west and more jobs in the cities. These were the nostrums of the Conservative Party, which under Sir John A. Macdonald surmounted its political disgrace after the Pacific Scandal of 1873 by exploiting economic discontent to turn out the unpopular Liberal government of Alexander Mackenzie (1873–78). Trumpeting tariff protection for industry and the jobs that industry brought, and promising prosperity just around the corner, Macdonald easily won the federal election of 1878.

The Conservatives promptly enacted a high tariff on imports – dubbed the National Policy by its creators – in 1879. Canada became and remained a high-tariff, protectionist country for most of the next century. The National Policy attracted investment from abroad, as its

creators intended, and produced factories and jobs, as well as gratitude
to the party that had made these things possible. The consumer paid, of
course, but consumers had yet to be organized into a political force.
Macdonald managed to be re-elected in 1882, 1887 and 1891 – each
time with a majority.

Protection was not merely advantageous, Macdonald's followers
argued, it was patriotic. A protective tariff kept out cheap American
goods and preserved Canadian investments (often by Americans) and

THE OLD FLAG.
THE OLD POLICY.
THE OLD LEADER.

An election poster of 1891 for Sir John A. Macdonald

Canadian jobs. In any case the Americans did it too (they did) and a high Canadian tariff was the only proper response. Indeed, the tariff traded on patriotism: keeping out American goods helped keep Canada British – though British goods paid the same duties as American. 'The Old Man, the Old Flag, the Old Party,' Conservatives sang: support Macdonald, save the Union Jack, and vote Conservative.

The real comment on Macdonald's policy was offered by those who voted, not with their ballots, but with their feet, leaving Canada for the theoretically obnoxious United States. This was not just true of English Canadians, culturally similar and English speaking, but of French Canadians as well. The English speakers melted into American society and in a generation or two were gone and forgotten, except as statistics, but the French speakers were more like European immigrants to the United States, clustering in their own sections of New England mill towns, worshipping in their own churches in their own language. At first the 'Canucks' (not intended as a complimentary term by their American neighbours) hoped to go home with what they had earned, but over time they stayed, and in such numbers that for a time in the early 1900s it seemed that large parts of New England might speak French rather than English. It was a fond dream, but fruitless. The Franco-Americans, as they were eventually, politely, called, changed language though not, usually, religion, and ethnicity eventually faded into folk memories.

The mass emigration of French Canadians disturbed the Catholic Church, which did all it could to encourage the faithful to stay in Quebec, or if they must go, to move into adjacent New Brunswick and Ontario. Remarkably, however, French Canadians did not choose to go further abroad, to distant Manitoba, where French was an official language. Instead, citizens of Ontario went west, in numbers sufficient to change the character of Manitoba and make it into a cultural replica of Ontario.

Language and Religion

Canadians only reluctantly made the difficult decision to live together in peace early in the nineteenth century. They did not believe that harmony was part of the deal. Religion was a vital force in society, and even if was impracticable for one religion to dominate or to drive out all the others, it was difficult for members of one sect to accept members of another as desirable neighbours. That was especially the case along the great divide between Protestants and Catholics, where it was theoretically possible to mobilize thousands or hundreds of thousands on behalf of a religious issue.

In the English-speaking provinces, and among English speakers in Quebec, Protestants grudgingly agreed in the 1840s and 1850s to pool their resources and to support a 'public' educational system that was really generically but unspecifically Protestant in all but name. The Catholics wished to establish their own education institutions and as part of the compromises that led to Confederation in 1867 they got their wish, trading tax-supported Protestant schools for the English in Quebec for tax-supported Catholic schools for Irish Catholics in Ontario. But only in Ontario.

In Manitoba or New Brunswick the compromise did not obtain, and the result was bitter disputes over minority rights for the French and Catholics in those two provinces in the 1870s and 1880s. In Manitoba feeling got so high that it overturned both official bilingualism and education in any language other than English. Accepting, perhaps unconsciously, the American belief that schools ought to educate for a common, homogeneous citizenship, Manitobans repeatedly voted for a single common school system and with it, they believed, an end to unpatriotic division.

Religion and schools were bad enough, but they were not something to go to war over. But just beside Manitoba, in the sparsely settled Northwest Territories, ethnicity and self-interest provoked a war.

The Northwest Rebellion

It was a small war but, as is often the case, it had large consequences. In its origins, it was a classic clash between local settlers and a distant and oblivious government. The settlers were white and Métis, both English and French speaking. The Métis brought with them a sense of grievance from Manitoba, where, they believed, they had been cheated of the rights and lands promised them in 1870. They also brought a memory of their leader in 1870, Louis Riel, who had forced the Canadian government to make terms, however badly those had later worked out. The Métis suggested calling back Riel to lead the discontented farmers of Saskatchewan, and to represent them to Ottawa. It was a bad idea, promptly adopted.

Riel returned to Canada from Montana, where he had been teaching in a school. He was not quite the man he had been in 1870. For one thing, he had a history of mental illness. For another, he had become convinced that he was a born-again Messiah, sent to lead his people by divine command. And finally, he, too, had a sense that his rights had been denied by a hostile Ottawa government, and he was determined, this time, to enforce them. The prime minister, Sir John A. Macdonald, was convinced that Riel was a self-seeking conniver, and was determined to have nothing to do with him. A clash was inevitable and it came.

Macdonald believed that he was dealing from a position of strength. Back in 1870 Red River was months away from central Canada, sheltered behind forests and lakes in a land with no roads and no railway. Then the Canadian government had no army to speak of, and it had to beg for help from the British. But in 1885 Macdonald had an army, though a small one, and no shortage of enthusiastic militia volunteers. Best of all, he could move them swiftly, for he had a railway. His Canadian Pacific project, under new direction, was nearing completion. A few gaps in the line could be easily overcome. Accordingly, Macdonald mobilized.

Riel struck first, ambushing a police patrol. This encouraged local Indians, with grievances of their own, to join him. Local Cree and Assiniboine attacked police posts and outlying settlers. Some settlers were killed – a further incentive to volunteers back in the east. Troops arrived promptly, and attacked Riel in the main Métis settlement of Batoche. Outnumbered and heavily outgunned, the Métis were defeated and scattered, while Riel was captured and put on trial for treason. Condemned, he was sentenced to death.

There was a case that Riel was insane and should not be considered responsible for his crimes. Even under nineteenth-century procedures,

Dead and wounded Métis, after their defeat by government forces at Batoche, during the Northwest Rebellion of 1885

this claim gave the government pause, and it sent a panel of doctors to examine the prisoner. Riel fiercely denied that he was mad, and the prospect of death by hanging seemed to hold no great terrors – and, indeed, he believed that he would rise on the third day after death. Sustained by the majority of the doctors, Macdonald resisted all pressures, which were considerable, because in Quebec Riel, as a man of French descent, was regarded by many as a martyr to English Canadian fanaticism. Macdonald replied, 'He shall hang though every dog in Quebec bark in his favour.' Hang he did, on 16 November 1885.

The Northwest Rebellion, more than the Red River Rebellion in 1870, became a symbol of the divide between English Canada and French Canada, which on the subject of Riel's guilt held diametrically opposed views. Could French Canadians expect justice from an Anglo-Saxon majority? Surely Riel's case proved the contrary. Should not Quebec, the only province where French was the majority language, increasingly look to its own interests and, possibly, its own defences? Many thought so, and even those who did not draw such a radical conclusion abandoned Macdonald and his Conservative Party.

As for the Métis, their cause was truly lost. They were not Indians, and they were not white. There was no special place for them, and they drifted on the margin of society – a society that in the west was dominated by English-speaking Protestants from Ontario. The Indians too had lost, though only a minority of the western tribes had participated in the rebellion. To the Indian peoples, the government applied its formula of treaties, land surrender and relegation to reserves. A system of residential schools was established to which Indian children were compulsorily sent, to learn the ways of civilization and to lose themselves in the larger assimilating society. Doubtful in theory, the residential schools were defective in practice: the kindest thing that may be said of them is that they failed in their purpose, creating citizens of a different hue whom the larger white society did not wish to receive.

The Sunny Years: 1896–1911

The crises over schools, language and race lasted well into the 1890s. Macdonald did not see the end of these problems, dying in June 1891, just after winning his last election. Over the next five years his Conservative Party produced four prime ministers and went down to defeat in the federal election of 1896.

The victor in that election was the Liberal Party, under Wilfrid Laurier, a Quebec politician and the first French Canadian to become Canadian prime minister. Laurier was a remarkable man, slim, elegant, flawlessly bilingual and a great orator in either official language. Laurier was, as he said himself, a classical Liberal on the British model. It was not calculated to make the Catholic Church in Quebec love him – in those years of conservative theology the church kept its distance from anything that smacked of liberalism and modernism.

Laurier was also a man of the nineteenth century, rather than the twentieth. He was endlessly quoted for shouting from the podium that 'The twentieth century belongs to Canada,' but Laurier's world was forever Queen Victoria's, a world where the globe was painted red, where Great Britain was truly great, and where Canada could cheerfully shelter behind British power. British power had the advantage, in Laurier's youth, of being distant but effective, barring the Atlantic to interfering European states, while keeping the Americans at least moderately impressed. And Britain was, on the whole, good in Laurier's eyes, even if certain local English Canadians were bad, or at least misguided, for wanting to snuggle up more closely to the British Empire. Laurier's Canada was a colonial Canada, a comfortable place where railways were built, mines dug and farms ploughed, a developing world whose business was its own, and no-one else's. It was not an imperial Canada, mobilizing to fight enemies around the world, under the direction and tutelage of statesmen from London. That might prove divisive, because most French Canadians thought of the empire as a good thing only as long as it did not interfere, or make trouble by taxing them or harvesting their children to serve in its armies. English Canadians, most of them, had no such reservations. Given the magnitude of the differences among English and French Canadians, not to mention the 20 years of economic disappointment since the 1870s, Laurier was determined to keep the empire a distant symbol, removed from Canadian life and politics. His point of view was understandable.

An example of the differences of the time was the question of 'temperance' – the regulation of the consumption of alcohol that in its more extreme forms meant the 'prohibition' of alcohol. Nineteenth-century Canada, English or French, was a hard-drinking place, with whisky the preferred drink. Reformers protesting an obvious social evil agitated for government action, and Laurier reluctantly obliged with a plebiscite in 1898. He knew that French Canada, where the prohibition movement was noisy but weak, was against and that English Canada was not strongly for temperance, and so it proved. The inconclusive results of his plebiscite gave the prime minister an excuse for doing nothing. But Laurier had not solved the question of temperance, merely postponed it: it would return to bedevil his successors in office.

It was ironic that Laurier was called to lead Canada at a time when the outside world was impinging to a greater degree than ever before. The Americans were a familiar problem, but a consistent one. The United States Congress was fiercely protectionist, rather like the Canadian Parliament, levying heavy and imaginative tariffs on behalf of established American interests. That hampered north-south trade and helped keep Great Britain in competition as a prime Canadian trading partner, as it fuelled a Canadian sense of a separate identity. Faced with high tariff barriers to the south, Laurier ostentatiously conferred a lower tariff on Great Britain and the British Empire.

London took this as a good sign. As it happened, a free-trading Great

Britain would not grant Canada a preferential tariff in return, but it did want Canadian cooperation in defence, either directly or in money. The notion was almost incomprehensible to Laurier and to many other Canadians: it was an inversion of the natural order of things. But Laurier's British counterparts argued that British strength was no longer sufficient to cow rival powers in Europe. As if to prove the point, when Britain became embroiled in a war in South Africa against two small Dutch settler republics, the enterprise was viewed with disapprobation if not utter hostility from France to Germany to Russia.

Canada sent troops to South Africa, rather against Laurier's wishes, so as to prevent a clash at home between English Canadian imperialists and French Canadian isolationists. The war was won, though not quickly, just in time for the coronation in 1902 of Queen Victoria's successor, Edward VII. Laurier (by then Sir Wilfrid) attended and used the occasion to fight off further schemes for imperial unity.

Immigration and The West

The next seven years were preoccupied with domestic developments. Immigrants arrived in a continuous stream, from Europe and the United States. The plains were settled in such numbers as to permit the establishment in 1905 of two new provinces, Saskatchewan and Alberta. The settlers were not, as before, mainly British but were drawn from Central and Eastern Europe, and they spoke Ukrainian, or Polish, or Russian, or Yiddish. Their children, especially in the cities, were enrolled in the homogenizing Canadian school system, which turned them, as far as possible, into English-speaking citizens.

There was virtually no French immigration either in this period or later, and even for immigrants arriving in the Canadian metropolis of Montreal, the temptation was overwhelming to gravitate to the English-speaking side of things. Though the French Canadian birthrate kept pace with immigration, French speakers mainly limited themselves to Quebec and adjacent parts of Ontario and New Brunswick. Though there were French islands in Saskatchewan, Alberta and even distant British Columbia, they remained small, almost unnoticed in the English-speaking sea.

The immigration created the Canadian breadbasket, the endless wheat fields that stretched from Manitoba to Alberta. Providentially, Canadian scientists developed a new strain of wheat that could be adapted to the short northern growing season, and soon the results were apparent. Engineering added grain elevators to the landscape – stubby country towers along the railway lines across the prairies, rows of concrete cones at the river and lake ports, proclaimed by the modernist architect Le Corbusier to be the ultimate expression of functional beauty in the twentieth century.

Wheat production rose steadily, from 42 million bushels in 1890; it was 56 million in 1900 and 394 million in 1915. To carry the wheat, Laurier enticed not one but two syndicates of capitalists to build transcontinental railways. It was a formidable enterprise for a country numbering only 5.4 million in 1901, but no-one expected the population to stay anywhere near that figure. Saskatchewan became, by 1911, Canada's third-largest province – helped in part by a steady trickle of Maritimers leaving the Atlantic Coast, so distant and restricted, for the opportunities of central and western Canada. (Prince Edward Island's population actually shrank in absolute numbers between 1891 and 1931.)

As long as prosperity lasted, it was possible to entertain the thought that Canada could pay for the Canadian Pacific, plus two new coast-to-coast railways. There was a sharp contraction in 1907, following a stock-market panic, but with that exception prosperity lasted until 1913. By then Canada's population had reached 7.6 million, including, it is estimated, 1.8 million immigrants. It was impressive, but to pay for Laurier's development schemes it was not enough.

The Great War

Laurier's government did not outlast the boom. It grew old and crotchety, addicted to patronage, responding only when prodded into action. It gave lip-service to the new progressive ideas of the early twentieth century, but apart from appointing a labour specialist with a PhD from Harvard, Mackenzie King, as labour minister, Laurier did nothing to satisfy the self-confident citizens of the new age. Perhaps that was because he was pushed from another direction – discontented farmers from the west who resented getting world prices for their wheat while paying high, 'protected' Canadian prices for the necessities of life.

This pressure Laurier could understand. He struck a deal with United States President W.H. Taft for a mutual tariff reduction (reciprocity) early in 1911. The Liberals presumed this would be universally popular, and they were happy to call an election on the issue. Instead they found themselves swept out of office by an anti-American tide in Ontario and an anti-British wave in Quebec (where Laurier was judged to have cooperated too much, too closely, with the British). American flags were hissed in silent movie theatres, and propagandists darkly prophesied that divorce and crime on the American model would be let loose in Canada if the tariff barrier were ever lowered.

THE FIRST WORLD WAR

The new prime minister was a Conservative from Nova Scotia, Sir Robert Borden. Borden headed a ramshackle alliance of English Canadian imperialists and French Canadian isolationists, which in ordinary times would have meant little. It was Borden's fate to be prime minister when the ultimate call of empire came, in August 1914, and it was not surprising that he and his government found the answer difficult to make.

Thanks to an eccentric defence minister, Sir Sam Hughes, a large Canadian expeditionary force was quickly raised and dispatched overseas in scenes of the utmost confusion. The ingenious Hughes equipped his troops with a Canadian-made hunting rifle, excellent for hunting, but unsuited for rapid firing and prone to jam in the mud of the battlefield. (He also patented, but fortunately did not manufacture, an entrenching shovel with a hole in the centre to allow marksmen to aim and fire from behind a 'protective' screen.)

Hughes at first feared that he and his troops would miss the war. When the British government hesitated for a day or two to declare war, even after the Germans invaded Belgium and France, a frustrated Hughes hauled down the Union Jack over his headquarters, declaring that he was ashamed to be British.

Mohawk volunteers for World War I

The Great War was fought in Belgium and France, as far as most Canadians were concerned, and ultimately 425,000 served overseas. (Scattered contingents also fought in North Russia and Siberia.) 'In Flanders Fields,' written by a Canadian officer, caught the spirit of melancholy (if not overly sentimental) determination that animated the troops who left 'row on row' of dead behind them – over 60,000 dead, out of an army of 619,000 and a population of 8.1 million in 1918.

Canadian troops saw large-scale battle first at Ypres, in Belgium, in April 1915, and ended the war at Mons, also in Belgium, during the final retreat of the German army, on 11 November 1918. Their most notable engagement was at Vimy Ridge in northern France in April 1917, where they drove strongly entrenched Germans from a commanding position over the Allied lines; a graceful memorial still stands on the spot, above a large cemetery.

Canadian troops knew a variety of commanders, British at first, but later Sir Arthur Currie, a Canadian general who before the war had been an unsuccessful real estate agent in Victoria, British Columbia. Currie and other commanders of the Canadian Corps served as a buffer between their troops and a British high command that had no better strategy than to batter at the German lines of trenches (punctuated by machine guns) in offensive after futile offensive; and the Germans returned the compliment. The trenches the Canadians knew snaked across the low-lying Flanders plain, close to sea level and in a rainy climate. 'General Mud,' one Canadian officer quipped, was the real commander of the battle.

At home the politicians did their best to feed the war with draft after draft of recruits and when the recruits dried up in 1917, with conscripts. Conscription proved intensely divisive in Canada, because French Canadians increasingly saw this war as not their war. Appeals to their French blood fell on deaf ears, for France was nothing more than a distant memory and, to a Catholic population, a country lamentably afflicted by atheism – worse than the English Canadians, who were after all Protestants.

Borden, whose parliamentary mandate had expired, was forced to call an election on the issue. Laurier's Liberals split over conscription, with most English Canadian Liberals supporting Borden. Borden formed a coalition government without a single elected French Canadian member. Conscription was duly passed, although enforcing it proved difficult. In some parts of the country, the authorities exempted practically everyone who appeared before them, and, to Borden's sorrow, conscription proved as desperately unpopular in rural areas as it was in French Quebec.

The war brought the return of prosperity, which had vanished suddenly in 1913. The unemployed found work, either as soldiers or in the munitions factories that sprang up across the country. Farmers found markets in Allied purchasing boards. Friends of the government, it was claimed, found profits, and the government's reputation (though not Borden's personally) was tarnished as a result. Crude economic policies resulted in rapid inflation, and inflation led to labour militancy and strikes. Divided by language, Canadians by 1918 were increasingly divided by economic interests or, as the Marxists claimed, by class.

The government found it necessary to introduce an income tax to help pay for the war, and to appeal for funds through bond drives – Victory Loans as they were called. To universal astonishment the Victory Loans were oversubscribed. Mostly, however, the government paid for the war through debt – $2.98 billion by 1919, compared to $0.75 billion in 1914.

Borden found it necessary to stoke the fires of enthusiasm with increasingly inflammatory rhetoric. Germany, from a mere international law breaker in 1914, became a country disfigured by militarism, cruelty and autocracy in 1918. The war was always a romantic crusade in the eyes of many, and in the words of government propagandists, but by 1918 it promised to transform the nature of society, both international and domestic. Verbiage of this kind was not limited to Canada, of course: it allowed Canadians to keep pace with the enthusiasm of Americans and their idealistic president, Woodrow Wilson, after the United States entered the war in April 1917 (and paid for it thereafter). Idealism associated with the war spirit rammed through a reform of the civil service in 1918, and finally secured the temperance agenda (domestic prohibition) in all provinces but Quebec by 1919.

The war ended in November 1918. Had it not been for the war, 1918 would be remembered in Canada as the year of Spanish influenza. The Spanish flu respected no boundaries and jumped oceans, decimating civilian populations from Texas to Baffin Island, and from Oslo to Ottawa. Some 20 million died around the world, including 50,000 Canadians.

MAKING PEACE

Throughout the war, Sir Robert Borden insisted to the British government that Canadian sacrifices demanded some share in the direction of the conflict. Had the war been short, or relatively costless, this would have remained windy rhetoric. But the war was long, and costly, and it had notably strained the resources of Great Britain itself. Canadian and Australian soldiers were crucial to the success of the British army on the Western Front, while Canadian money financed the last two years of British munitions purchases in Canada.

It was a less dependent Canada that Borden represented at the Paris Peace Conference of 1919, called to draft a treaty of peace with defeated Germany. Borden and Canada appeared at the conference in a dual role, as a nation that had fought in the war, and as part of the British Empire. Borden found that he was far more influential in the latter role than in the former, helping settle Balkan boundaries, or regulating navigation on the Danube. In return for Canadian cooperation during the conference, and for the symbolic value of a united, powerful empire, the British prime minister, Lloyd George, helped secure international recognition for Canada as a relatively important belligerent (relative to, say, Portugal or Serbia or Belgium), and as an entity that deserved reward for its sacrifices during the war.

The Paris Peace Conference, in addition to dictating terms of peace to Germany and its allies, also established a League of Nations, an international body whose function was to keep the peace by preventing or regulating disputes among nations. Canada became an autonomous member of the League, entitled to send its own delegates to international meetings, if desired.

Borden bore the treaty with Germany home and had it ratified by the Canadian Parliament in September 1919. It was not a pleasant experience. Some opposition members loudly wondered why Canada should keep the peace through the new League of Nations. Canada had had enough foreign affairs for the time being, one western member of Parliament claimed; it should in future tend to itself first. Part way through the debate Borden had a nervous collapse that sent him off on a prolonged vacation. When he returned to Ottawa in the summer of 1920, he quickly resigned.

Changes, Social and Economic

The Canada of 1919 was very different from the Canada of Borden's youth, and even more Laurier's. It was much larger in population (8.3 million compared to 3.7 million in 1871) and it was much richer. In Canada in 1875 there were no electric lights, only gas or, more usually, kerosene to lighten the darkness of long northern winter nights. Streetcars, the few that there were, were horsedrawn. Some city streets were paved, but roads outside the cities were more obstacles to be endured than highways to travel. The railway and the steamboat were the sum total of convenient transportation, and for the centre of the continent, from the Great Lakes to the Pacific, they did not exist.

The world of 1919 was considerably altered. City travel was much easier on electric street railways. It was even possible to travel from Toronto to Buffalo or Cleveland using streetcars and from Toronto to distant Halifax or Edmonton or Vancouver using coal-burning railways. Highways, it was true, were still something of a fable, but gradually paved roads were snaking out from the cities. Propelling the demand for paved highways was the automobile, usually imported from the United States, but sometimes made locally, either in American-owned factories (Ford in Windsor, Ontario) or in Canadian-owned companies (McLaughlin in Oshawa, Ontario).

The sounds and smells of Victorian cities were receding – the clopping of horses, the rattle of steel wheels on carriages or wagons, the wafting of horse manure. Pioneers of the automobile age argued that the automobile made cities quieter and in some senses that was quite true. There was the new sound of the telephone ringing – telephones had first been proven to work in Brantford, Ontario in 1876, a fact that Canadians, as opposed to Americans, who also claimed the honour, were prone to emphasize. The telephone's inventor, the Scots-born Alexander Graham Bell, gave his name to an American company, Bell Telephone, which migrated north to dominate telephones in Quebec and Ontario until the 1990s.

Luxury cars apart, Canadians opted for American models and like Americans, Canadians opted to drive on the right with their steering wheels on the left. It was another sign, and not an insignificant one, of cultural influences drifting over the border.

The psychological effects of the war are the most difficult to measure, or to distinguish from other, larger cultural influences. There is not much doubt that the Victorian age, with its emphasis on conformity and respectability and stability, came to an end sometime in the first or second decade of the twentieth century. It may have taken longer to die in Canada because, as a distant and semi-colonial society, distance and dependence insulated the country. Subversive ideas, carried in books and magazines, were assumed to come from New York or London or Paris, and they originated in Canada only in very small part. Nor did travel and tourism play much part: only a tiny minority could afford voyages abroad, and of those who did leave the country many never returned.

Most Canadians before or after the war were never directly exposed to modern art or new styles in music. There were no symphony orchestras, and art galleries were few and their collections more respectable than interesting. Canada produced no musicians of international calibre who could afford to stay home, and the same was true of acting and film making (though Mack Sennett, the director, and Mary Pickford, the actress, were both Canadian.) In art, however, a Toronto-based collection of artists calling themselves the Group of Seven revolutionized the portrayal of the Canadian landscape, extending Canadians' notions of themselves into a sense of the wilderness. (Some of the Group went on to become notable war artists – a different kind of wilderness—in the service of the government.)

Suddenly, between 1914 and 1918, hundreds of thousands of Canadians found themselves travelling. While Canadians at home were closing down saloons and banning the import of wine, young Canadians abroad were sampling wine and spirits, many for the first time, and smoking, a vice frowned upon in virtuous circles at home. Parents were shocked to find their returned soldier sons were swearing, smoking and, in defiance of the law, drinking. And not only sons.

Women's status changed too during the war, but also as part of a much longer process. As in the rest of the western world, women were disenfranchised in Canada, their role in society relegated to the home or to a limited number of service professions. In Quebec especially, though to a limited degree elsewhere, women could escape some of the limits on their activities by accepting orders and entering convents, but that was an option not open to most. Very gradually, in the late nineteenth century, women obtained access to higher education including medicine and law, but these remained a tiny percentage of the female population. In agriculture – where women performed a substantial part of the work – there were women's auxiliaries and women's institutes. Nationally there was the National Council of Women, encouraged if not inspired by the wife of one of the governors general, Countess Aberdeen.

Following the British and American examples, agitation for the grant of the vote to women (female suffrage) grew in the decade before the war. But it was the war, where the domestic war effort depended so much on women's voluntary service as well as on women's paid labour, which finally broke down male resistance. Women got the vote in Manitoba, Saskatchewan and Alberta in 1916 and in Ontario in 1917.

Nationally, wives and sisters of soldiers got the vote in time to vote for conscription in the 1917 election; all women got the vote the following year.

The war also brought changes to the relations of labour and business. Labour organizations had long existed in Canada and labour unions were legalized in the 1870s. The trade union movement was divided regionally and ideologically, with a substantial radical and Marxist fringe, especially in western Canada. It was the war, however, that accelerated the industrialization of Canada and that accelerated, because of run-away inflation, the growth of radical sentiment. There was, as well, the example of the Russian Revolution of 1917 that gave proponents of the notion of a separate working class a model to work for – and the authorities a dreadful example to work against. In 1919 labour unrest resulted in an attempt at a general strike in Winnipeg, interpreted by the government as the first step in a Communist revolution. Strike leaders were arrested and the strike suppressed, and the hopes and fears of the moment passed. Nevertheless, there was the sense on both sides that something was possible in the future – something that before the war would have been unimaginable.

Instead of solving society's problems, as Borden had hoped, the war created many more.

CHAPTER FIVE

Depression and War, 1919–45

The history of Canada from 1919 to 1945 is the story of a single generation. It is a history of economic oscillations, national contradictions and political confusion. Raised in the apparent security of the pre-war British Empire, tested by the disruptions of World War I, the young men and women of 1919 hoped that peace would bring stability. Indeed it would: only it was the peace of 1945, not that of 1919, that seemed to answer the questions and finally fulfill the aspirations of the generation that had passed through 'the war to end all wars.'

Affluence: The 1920s

The 1920s began with a savage depression. In the cities, bread lines formed outside welfare offices; in the country families struggled to make ends meet in a world that had no use, or at any rate no price, for their products. Governments grudgingly doled out money, as little as possible, to meet the need.

Then, suddenly, the depression was over and sunny economic times smiled on Canada. Woodpulp was in demand by American publishers, Canadian wheat fetched a high price, and Canadian minerals fed the thriving industries of the United States. Canadian industry too found markets, for its furniture, its automobiles, its shoes. City governments paved streets and built schools – modern, bright buildings, sometimes with the hitherto unheard-of luxury of swimming pools. Provincial governments built highways and paved them. Toronto and Montreal were linked by paved road for the first time, and then Toronto and

Ottawa. The federal government laid low, lowered taxes and started to pay off the war debt.

The 1920s were an age of building. Canada's first skyscrapers rose, though to much more modest heights than their American models. Toronto and Montreal ran an informal competition, which aroused intense interest, for the tallest building, not only in Canada, but in the British Empire. The Bank of Commerce in Toronto (34 stories, or 477 feet, completed in 1931) won the race, dwarfing the Royal Bank of Canada in Montreal (1928 and 392 feet). In Vancouver there was the Marine Building (21 stories, 1930), and there was even a miniature example in Quebec City. All these buildings showed the prosperity of the times.

The leaders of society were secular. Business and businessmen dominated the decade, and set its tone. In Toronto, newspaper readers followed the adventures of the local department store magnate, Sir John Eaton; in Montreal it was the utility magnate and banker, Sir Herbert Holt. Mining engineers dug wealth out of the rock of the Canadian Shield and shipped it to the great cities. Electrical engineers built generating stations (vast echoing spaces, behind a façade of art deco) at Niagara Falls. The St Lawrence was dammed, and the Saguenay, and the Stave Fall dam was opened in 1911 in British Columbia. Low taxes and high profits gave confidence to the business class. And, indisputably, the general population was profiting too: the rising total of automobiles on Canadian roads, and the modest single-family brick houses spreading through the new suburbs showed how much.

The monuments of the decade were secular. The early 1900s had been a great age of church building, appropriate to a society where attendance at church was the custom of the many, and abstention from public worship the privilege of the daring few, or of the many poor. The skylines of Toronto or Montreal before 1914 were a forest of church spires; their skylines by 1930 had a downtown core of banks and hotels and offices thrusting upwards, dwarfing the towers of religion.

This is not to say that piety was not in evidence during the 1920s. The prime minister of the day prayed beside his mother's grave, with a *Toronto Star* scribe in close attendance. *Star* readers got the news, and the message, the next day, in their tens of thousands. Canadians read Sinclair Lewis's *Babbitt* with a shock of recognition – where they could get it. (*Babbitt* dealt with the stuffiness and hypocrisy of society in a small American town – not far from the Canadian border either geographically or spiritually.) *Babbitt* at least could pass the censors, who were an active breed in interwar Canada, and especially active in Quebec, where secular authority was reinforced by the Catholic Index of prohibited books. In painting the Group of Seven's vivid canvases attracted as much derision as praise.

MACKENZIE KING

Canadians did not know that the prime minister of the day also believed that he talked to the spirits of the dead, and he sought their reassuring counsel in seances. William Lyon Mackenzie King (1874–1950) was the son of a Toronto lawyer and law professor and the grandson, through his mother, of William Lyon Mackenzie, the incendiary rebel of the 1830s. Mackenzie had thrived on invective and disruption; King preferred dullness, stability and predictability. Mackenzie King could not have been more different from his grandfather, a fact that did not prevent him from venerating the old man's memory.

King was a thoroughly modern late Victorian. Trained as a lawyer, he dipped also into social work and then academia, taking a PhD in economics at Harvard (where, somewhat later, he was offered the chair in economics). King made his mark as a labour expert, and Sir Wilfrid Laurier recognized the fact by making him Canada's first minister of labour, in 1909. Laurier recognized something else about King: his driving ambition, and a self-regard that allowed him to rationalize his frequent self-doubts and to arrive at solutions that he could justify to the world, and to his diary. (King's diary, more than 50 years of it, survives and is the foundation of a thriving Mackenzie King industry.)

After Laurier was defeated in the 1911 federal election, King was offered employment by the Rockefeller family in the United States, which needed advice on its mismanaged labour relations. Successful in the task, King was enriched in reputation and money, which he needed when, in 1919, Sir Wilfrid Laurier died.

King had not followed other English Canadian Liberals out of the

William Lyon Mackenzie King, the prime minister who 'did nothing by halves that he could do by quarters'

party on the issue of conscription. As an ex-minister, and as a party member loyal to Sir Wilfrid, King commended himself to the French Canadian wing of the party. It was enough: he won the leadership at a party convention in August 1919 (Canada's first political leadership convention) and two years later he was prime minister, defeating Borden's hapless successor, Arthur Meighen.

King had learned the lesson of the divisive war years. Canada needed political stability, he believed, and that meant, first and foremost, political unity between English and French Canadians. A close second, among King's priorities, was a tactical sense that exalted caution and consensus. Mackenzie King's style as a political leader was the way of the turtle, slow moving but long-lived. Many of his opponents, and his supporters too, found to their cost that turtles can bite.

King's governments in the 1920s were slow moving. His main objective was political: while keeping French Canadians firmly within the Liberal Party, he wished to expand to the west, and attract farm voters back to the Liberals. By a mixture of sound finance (keeping the debt down), cautious tariff cuts (appealing to farmers) and isolationist rhetoric (conciliating French Canadians) as well as an opportunistic sense of tactics, King achieved his goal. He even turned a narrow defeat in the 1925 election into victory, when he won fewer seats than the Conservatives did but kept office with the support of minor parties.

Then, after a brief sojourn in opposition, he resoundingly defeated the Conservatives in another election in 1926.

King did nothing by halves that he could do by quarters, a poet once quipped, and it was true that King's 1920s were not exciting times, and perhaps not even interesting times. The curse of interesting times appeared with double force just in time for the 1930s.

Canada in the Great Depression

In the 1930s almost everything that could go wrong with the Canadian economy did. Deflation, drought and bankrupt cities: these were only a few manifestations of a decade of despair and frustration. It took ten years for the nation's economy to produce as much wealth as it had in 1929 – and at its worst, the gross domestic product was a scant 50 per cent of what it had been at the end of the twenties. 'The Dirty Thirties' were unusual in the duration of the crisis, and in its variety. The decade was especially important for its effects on society and for the memories it left behind. After World War I, the Great Depression was the second critical event of the century – the one that shook the economic certainties as surely as the Great War had undermined the assurances of politics and culture.

The depression began with a fall in wheat prices. Canada was a wheat-exporting country and the three prairie provinces, Manitoba, Saskatchewan and Alberta, depended on the profitable sale of the wheat crop. But wheat was in surplus around the world, and prices fell – not once but consistently until by 1932 they reached $0.54 a bushel. (The price had been $1.46 in 1927.) Then there were the falls in pulp and paper prices – the mainstay of the near north. The value of pulp and paper production fell from $244 million in 1929 to $123 million in 1933. And so it went, in industry after industry.

The Canadian government applied the traditional remedy and raised tariffs, but not enough in the minds of the electorate, which in 1930 returned the Conservatives under R. B. Bennett to office. Bennett promised to use the tariff 'to blast a way into the markets of the world,' and he did, indeed, raise the tariff. The markets of the world were unimpressed, the more so because every country was trying the same remedy, which amounted to trying to export the economic downturn somewhere, anywhere, else. 'Beggar my neighbour' was the generic term applied to these policies, and it was apt enough.

The futility of Bennett's policies was apparent by 1932, the lowest year of the depression in Canada. Nevertheless he hosted, in a steaming Ottawa summer, a great British Empire economic conference that decided to confer lower rates of duty on goods traded within the empire, from Samoa to Scotland. Canada's concessions were few, and those few picayune, but in return Canada got lower duties in the all-important British market – all-important because American tariffs were now so high that Canadian exports south were in danger of strangulation.

The 'Ottawa agreements' did have another positive effect: they impressed the Americans, who in any case had drawn their own conclusions about the uselessness of sky-high tariffs. (The American economy, too, had fallen by 50 per cent, measured by gross domestic product.) For the next decade American policy aimed to get around, or even totally abolish, the Ottawa duties.

Thanks to the penny-pinching policies of the Mackenzie King government in the 1920s, Ottawa enjoyed a good credit rating in the 1930s. This happy circumstance allowed Bennett to bail out province after province. Three provinces, Alberta, Saskatchewan and New Brunswick were almost literally bankrupt, and only aid from Ottawa prevented them from reneging on their creditors. Most of the rest of the provinces were in poor shape, and help from the federal government was most welcome.

The main item in provincial budgets was relief for the unemployed in the cities, and for farmers impoverished by the collapse of agricultural markets. In Ontario, which suffered less from the depression than other provinces because its economy was diversified among mining, forestry, agriculture and manufacturing, not all of which were hit at the same time, many rural doctors were paid in eggs and chickens, and some rural teachers worked for subsistence. Across the land, the unemployed were put to work, sometimes doing productive tasks like building highways and airfields, and sometimes not, being set to things such as scything the grass in municipal parks. Always there was a stigma to being unemployed, something that those who experienced it never forgot.

Not everyone suffered. Deflation lowered prices even faster than employers could cut wages. As a result, those with jobs were likely to do well, or better, and those jobs included more than the middle class. Automobile-manufacturing cities such as Oshawa, outside Toronto, and mining communities such as Timmins (a gold-mining city at a time when the price of gold was rising) did better than the average. Nor was the depression the same for everyone across all ten years of the 1930s. The slide was slow at first, and recovery began by 1934 in most of the country. Somewhere, somehow, Canadians found the wherewithal to buy consumer goods in all but the very worst of the depression. To take a couple of examples, Canada manufactured twice as many radios in 1937 as in 1929, and by 1939 there were 250,000 more automobiles on Canadian roads than in 1929 – and more roads too.

The worst was reserved for the plains, where poverty was followed by a kind of biblical plague. Drought shrivelled the crops and then destroyed the soil, which blew away in dust clouds in 1936 and 1937. City dwellers could feel the soil on their teeth, and see it on the horizon, swirling. There were locusts too, in case the drought spared anything. Farmers harnessed their horses to the automobiles they had bought in the days of prosperity, and for which they could no longer afford gas. These cars were derisively called 'Bennett buggies.'

Bennett's relations with the provinces were also poisonous. Bennett was a man of genuinely superior intelligence, but he coupled this quality with an overweening arrogance. As paymaster to the provinces, the prime minister made sure that they begged for every last penny he doled out. Not surprisingly, by 1935 he was at odds with virtually every one, and his Conservative Party had lost every single provincial election in the previous three years. Admittedly, some of the provincial leaders thrown up by the depression, especially in Ontario, Quebec and Alberta, were themselves difficult if not bizarre personalities who would have tried the patience of a saint; and Bennett was no saint.

Bennett worried too that radical political movements might become a force. There was plenty of agitation, against unemployment, against the economic system. There had been, since 1921, a Canadian Communist Party and in 1932 a democratic socialist party, the Co-operative Commonwealth Federation (CCF) was formed. The Communists had some influence, and plenty of active organizers, in the labour movement and among the unemployed. They even organized in 1935 an 'On to Ottawa Trek,' which seriously perturbed Bennett. In a riot in Regina, the capital of Saskatchewan, one policeman was killed. Some marchers reached Ottawa, and talked and paraded and then went home.

Canadians' sympathies may have been with the marchers, but their votes were not. Mackenzie King was still waiting in the wings, and it was to this odd, dumpy little man that the electorate turned. The prime minister's political goose was cooked. Obliged by the constitution to call an election in October 1935, Bennett's Conservative Party was almost annihilated. Bennett retired to England, where he entered the House of Lords. He never returned to Canada.

Back in office was the inevitable Mackenzie King. 'It's King or Chaos,' Liberal Party propagandists told the electorate, and faced with that choice the voters took King. King had no idea how to cure the depression; luckily for him he did not have to.

THE DOMINION AND THE DICTATORS

Foreign policy was one area where King felt at home. Fearing the impact on Canadian national unity of another British-led European war, he steadily resisted any and all pressures from the British government to lend his support to the details of their policy. In so doing, in 1926, he secured British recognition that Canada and the other dominions of the British Empire (Ireland, Australia, New Zealand and South Africa) had the right to manage their own foreign policies. Five years later, in 1931, this was embodied in a British law, the Statute of Westminster. In all things except the amendment of the Canadian constitution, the British North America Act of 1867, Canada now had full autonomy or even, though the word was not used, independence. (The constitution remained subject to British parliamentary action because the federal government and the provinces could not agree on how to amend it.)

There was one qualification to King's quest for autonomy. 'If a great and clear call of duty ever comes,' he said in 1923, 'Canada will be at Britain's side.' In other words, things had changed, but they hadn't changed that much. King knew that English Canadian public opinion would still demand participation in any war that threatened Britain's independence or existence. The British government chose not to listen and for most of the twenties and thirties believed that King was a closet republican, not to be relied on in a crisis; but that was precisely when King could be relied on.

King, it must be admitted, did lend credence to this misinterpretation. He had been educated at Harvard, and he told the American envoy in Ottawa in 1935 that he was known to prefer 'the American road.' He signed a trade agreement with the United States, lowering tariffs, immediately on taking office for his third administration, and signed another, along with an agreement with Great Britain, in 1938.

King played a careful game in foreign policy, balancing distance from Great Britain with his growing fear that war was, after all, inevitable. Adolf Hitler had come to power in Germany in 1933, and his actions were well reported in Canada. King would have had to be a fool to ignore the portents, and King, though he sometimes concealed it, was not a fool. Yet he knew that premature commitments, before public opinion was ready, would upset the precarious political balance between English and French Canadians.

In 1935 Canada drew back from League of Nations oil sanctions against Italy, which had invaded Ethiopia. (Ironically, the Canadian delegate had proposed the oil sanctions, only to have his government repudiate him.) 'Sanctions,' a Canadian official opined, were 'Swiss for War.' At an imperial conference in London in 1937, King steadfastly refused to commit Canada to any particular course of action to help Britain. He went on to visit Germany, had tea with Hitler, whom he described in his diary as a 'simple German peasant,' but simultaneously warned Hitler's ministers that if it came to war, Canada would be at Britain's side.

In the meantime, King fervently supported the appeasement policies of Neville Chamberlain, the British prime minister, as he attempted to satisfy Germany and avoid war. King approved of appeasement both because it held out the hope, however faint, that there would be no war, but also because it made plain that in any war with Germany the fault could not conceivably lie with Great Britain.

On the other side of the ocean, King was a frequent visitor to Washington, where he stayed with Franklin D. Roosevelt, the American president. Both men pretended they had known each other since university days (Roosevelt too had gone to Harvard). That was not true, but in fact the two men got on exceedingly well. Roosevelt liked Canada, and he liked King, but more importantly he believed that there would be another European war and that the United States must look to its defences. Canada was part of his defence vision, for the American Atlantic Coast could not be defended without Canadian cooperation.

In 1938 president and prime minister exchanged public pledges that they would cooperate in defence: just in time, because by 1938 Adolf Hitler's Germany was on the move. In September 1939 Hitler invaded Poland. Great Britain and France declared war on Germany on 3 September, and Canada followed with its own, separate declaration of war on 10 September. All but a handful of members of parliament, including almost all French Canadians in the House of Commons, voted for the declaration.

How had this happened? King had carefully prepared the way. His French Canadian supporters knew that he was not irrationally pro–British or pro-war: they trusted his judgement. They knew, as King did, that English Canada would refuse to remain neutral in any conflict, and they decided to trust to King's leadership to ensure that if there had to be a war, there would at least be no conscription, as in 1917. King promised, and the leaders of all the other political parties promised too. The promise was ratified in a snap general election in March 1940, which confirmed King and his Liberals in office with another huge majority in parliamentary seats.

THE WAR AT HOME

This electoral victory of 1940 was crucial to the five years of war that followed. King could beat off a toothless parliamentary opposition and rely on his solid majority to support him in disputes with the provinces. He used it to appropriate virtually all economic power, including taxation, permissible under the constitution in cases of emergency or war.

King relied on an exceptionally strong cabinet – powerful personalities who were often political powers in their own right. C. D. Howe, his minister of munitions, converted the economy to a war footing, producing everything from shells to trucks to bombers. Howe, a Liberal, recruited the largely Conservative business class to be his executives and managers, which further undermined the Conservative parliamentary opposition. Demands for a 'national' (i.e. business and Conservative) government faded. By the fall of 1941 Canada had full employment, at which point the King government slapped on stringent wage and price controls, thereby avoiding the inflation and consequent labour unrest that had disfigured the war effort in World War I.

Howe and his executives controlled virtually every aspect of economic life. They built aircraft factories, ammonia plants, and shipyards. Little or nothing was left to private choice. 'If the product is not needed, the plant should not be built,' Howe remarked in 1941. Nor would it be.

Not all the consequences were easy. Some products had to be controlled, both to fuel war production and to reserve necessary supplies for Great Britain, besieged by a German submarine campaign and cut off from its European supplies by the German conquest of most of the continent in 1940–41. Gas, rubber tyres, coal, butter, meat, tea and coffee, among other things, were rationed. Stringent taxation and

A naval convoy in Halifax harbour in 1942

compulsory savings programmes paid for as much of the war as the economy could stand, and postponed demand until later. Despite this, because of full employment at newly-created factory jobs, the average Canadian family actually did better – real consumption per head rose from $731 in 1938 to $992 in 1945 (all figures in current dollars).

The Canadian government could finance only so much of the war from taxes. Like its predecessor in World War I, the government borrowed, to pay for a government deficit that went from $2 million in 1939 to $1.9 billion in 1944. But almost two thirds of the new debt was financed by the sale of 'Victory Bonds' to the public – $9 billion out of $14 billion. Thanks to inflation controls, interest costs were much lower than in the previous war.

Much of the Canadian war effort depended on imports from the United States. Coal, oil, machine tools and aircraft engines – all had to be imported. American dollars were carefully husbanded through stringent foreign-exchange controls. That was not enough: Canada needed something to sell to the Americans, and in large quantities. The opportunity was afforded by the United States' delayed entry into the war, which meant that American armament programmes lagged about 18 months behind their Canadian counterparts. An agreement in April 1941 gave the Americans free access to Canadian armaments factories, effectively integrating the two countries' arms procurement policies. As a result, Canadian reserves of American dollars soared, and worries that Canada might not have enough money to buy coal to power factories or heat homes vanished.

All in all, Canada's directed war economy was a success. As important, it was recognized as such. Canada moved from unemployment to full employment to labour shortages. The government mobilized the workforce, avoided serious inflation, placed no strain on living standards and distributed burdens and benefits in a way that most people considered fair. At the same time, the government had sidelined the provinces. The war was indisputably Ottawa's business, and the provinces, with their mandate to build schools and roads, and to look after (now non-existent) welfare rolls, had little to say about it. Without quite intending to, Mackenzie King had become master of a nearly unitary state, in which all essential decisions were taken in Ottawa, by himself or his ministers or their executives, styled 'the mandarins' by an admiring press.

Canadians considered their war effort impressive. Certainly it was, by national standards. Even internationally Canadian war production was significant: Canadian trucks, for example, were a significant proportion of the Allied total. Canadian war production ranked third among the Allies, after the United States and Great Britain. That said, taken as a percentage of three countries' war production total, the United States accounted for 60, Great Britain for 35, and Canada, 5 per cent. All this, it should be noted, from a population one-fifth the size of Britain's, and one-tenth that of the United States.

Canadians had sacrificed much to attain the figure of 5 per cent, but the sacrifice conferred a 'respectable' rather than a 'directing' role among the Allies. This, fortunately, was something the Canadian government understood.

The War Abroad

After the war was over, Mackenzie King made much of the fact that he more than any other Canadian was known and respected abroad. To his diary, King confided that of all the leaders of the world in office in 1939, only he and Josef Stalin of the Soviet Union were still in place when the war ended in 1945. (He did not add that Stalin's methods of maintaining himself in power were rather different from King's.) The prime minister lost no opportunity to bask in association with American president Roosevelt or British prime minister Churchill, and partly for that purpose, King hosted them at two conferences in Quebec City, in 1943 and 1944. The photographs of the three leaders sitting on a terrace overlooking the broad St Lawrence were most effective, both for what they told and what they did not tell. Canadians did not know that once the pictures were taken Mackenzie King retired and allowed the two more senior and powerful leaders to do their necessary business of directing the war alone.

King did not wish to leave the matter of Allied support to chance. He had a difficult task, expanding the economy, squeezing the taxpayer and feeding the military. With the economy more or less under the control of his ministers, it was the military that absorbed most of his personal attention.

To judge by the results, the Canadian military war record was considerable. Out of a population of roughly 12 million, 1.1 million Canadians – men and women – saw service in uniform between 1939 and 1945. Not all were in the armed forces at the same time: at their peaks, respectively, the army totalled 496,000, the navy 92,000, and the air force 206,000.

The army was designed, from the beginning, to serve overseas. A first division left Canada in December 1939, and a second division soon followed. Ultimately, five divisions went overseas, three infantry and two armour. To house these units, first a corps and then an army (First Canadian Army) were created.

In the air, Canada contributed a training establishment that graduated 131,000 aircrew for the whole British Empire between 1940 and 1945. Canadians served in all aspects of the air war, from coastal patrols to fighters to heavy bombers. Some worked directly in the British Royal Air Force, while 46 squadrons were deployed under the Royal Canadian Air Force. The RCAF was in some respects a glamorous service, and also a perilous one because of the heavy casualties in bombing raids over Germany.

Finally, there was the navy. The pre-war Royal Canadian Navy was tiny, but it was on that basis that a larger force had to be created. The strain sometimes showed, and though the Canadian effort at sea was significant both in numbers and role, until 1943 the navy was not as effective as it should have been. At the height of the Battle of the Atlantic against German submarines, the Canadians had to be withdrawn for retraining. Thereafter they served effectively, but the question lingers as to why so much time had elapsed before this drastic action had to be taken.

Mackenzie King expected that most casualties would be in the army, as in World War I. In a curious way fortune smiled upon him for the first four years of the war, because with two exceptions no Canadian army units were seriously engaged against the enemy until July 1943. The first two Canadian divisions arrived too late in Britain to be more than perfunctorily engaged in the disastrous land campaign in Belgium and France in the spring of 1940. While the British suffered large casualties and lost most of their equipment to the Germans before being evacuated to England from Dunkirk, the Canadian formations were more or less intact. Had the Germans then invaded England in the fall of 1940, the Canadian army might have been heavily engaged. But as it happened, the Germans did not invade, and the Canadians spent the next few years defending the south coast of England against an enemy who never came.

In the autumn of 1941 it was clear that war in Europe would be accompanied by war in the Far East. Japan, once an ally of Great Britain (and Canada) threatened war against the British Empire and the United States. In anticipation and in a feeble sign of deterrence, Winston Churchill asked Mackenzie King for some troops to defend Hong Kong. King, believing that the threat was not imminent, sent some units still in training. In this case, a futile gesture resulted in futile sacrifice. The Japanese attacked Hong Kong at the same time they attacked the American fleet at Pearl Harbor. Hong Kong and its largely Canadian garrison surrendered on Christmas Day, and the survivors spent the next four years in brutal captivity. The last stage of the battle for Hong Kong took place between competing British and Canadian histories, in which each blamed the other for the debacle.

The key event was not Hong Kong, of course, but Pearl Harbor, which guaranteed that the United States, hitherto clinging to frayed neutrality, would join the war. In Ottawa, at a Sunday lunch party, staid civil servants broke into song, and danced around their host's dinner table: henceforth, they knew, the Allies could not lose.

Winning meant invading Europe and driving the German armies back to Germany. The first stage of winning was to test German defences in France, and so in August 1942 a reconnaissance in force was sent across the English Channel to attack the port of Dieppe. It was not a happy occasion. The expedition was both misconceived and badly handled. Out of 5,000 men landed at Dieppe, 2,000 were taken prisoner, and another 1300 were killed or wounded. As at Hong Kong, the next 40 years were taken up with retrospective combat, with the

Canadians by and large blaming inept and self-serving British leadership and the British blaming incompetent Canadian commanders or, possibly, poorly trained troops.

The Canadian army went on to play a role in the successive invasions of Sicily and Italy in the summer of 1943, and in the D-Day invasion of Normandy, on 6 June 1944. The fighting in France was especially fierce, and casualties mounted at a rate greater than the trench warfare of World War I. Canadian troops fought bravely, and decisively in some instances, such as the Battle of the Scheldt in November 1944, but again their leadership was heavily criticized. Some commentators have concluded that in fact the Canadian army was better led under the amateur soldiers of World War I than under the professional generals of World War II, and the criticism has some justice.

The casualties of the summer and fall of 1944 produced a political crisis at home in October and November. Since 1939 Mackenzie King had ducked and weaved on conscription. In the crisis of 1940, King with virtually unanimous support (including Quebec) introduced it for home defence only. When Japan joined the war in December 1941 the resulting home-defence conscripts were sent (mostly) to British Columbia to await the Japanese invasion. They sat for two years, phantom soldiers derisively labelled 'zombies' after the undead monsters of West Indian fable. Then in April 1942 King used a plebiscite to release the government from its absolute pledge not to send conscripts overseas – a vote that revealed that French and English Canada stood on opposite sides of the issue. In 1942, Dieppe apart, there were no casualties and hence no need, and King postponed the issue until circumstances forced his hand.

Finally, after resignations from the cabinet on both sides of the issue, King reluctantly imposed conscription in 1940 for overseas service in November 1944. His party, though strained, did not break: enough French Canadian Liberals supported the prime minister, praising his obvious reluctance to do the distasteful but inevitable thing. Quebec nationalists grumbled and stored away a grievance for the future; but at the time there were remarkably few repercussions.

War's Consequences

The end of World War II found the Canadian army deep in Holland. A Canadian general took the German surrender there on 5 May 1945, and the Canadian liberation of the Netherlands formed a bond between these two relatively unimportant countries.

There was still the war against Japan, but that came to an end before any Canadian troops could be shipped across the Pacific. Canada participated, in a minor way, in the ending of the Japanese war, because a Canadian factory had refined the uranium that the Americans dropped, in bomb form, on the Japanese cities of Hiroshima and Nagasaki. Canada had participated in aspects of what was mainly an Anglo-American enterprise, but as a result Canada counted, temporarily, as one of the three countries with some knowledge of the 'atomic secret.'

Canada enjoyed a temporary prominence in many fields at the end of the war. Canada was solvent, for one thing, and its currency was convertible against the American dollar. In a world of blocked currencies, this was nearly unique. The Canadian navy was the world's fourth largest, as was the air force. The army had played a larger role in the final battles in Europe than, say, the French and Italian armies.

The war also brought about a reduction in Britain's status, economically and politically and in the long run militarily too. The British had depended on Canada, as in World War I, for supplies and loans, and there is no doubt the two countries were differently positioned, in their mutual relations, than they had been in 1939. Yet up to half a million Canadians, almost 5 per cent of the Canadian population, had spent the war years in Great Britain. They brought home with them a contingent of 48,000 war brides, 22,000 children, and memories that were, generally, favourable. In Sicily, Italy and northwestern Europe, Canadian soldiers fought as part of a larger British army, as Canadian airmen and sailors formed part of British air and sea fleets.

Relations with the Americans were different – closer in many respects, yet distant in others. Economically Canada depended during the war and thereafter on trade with the United States. Sales to Britain were still large if not larger, but they were financed on credit: only the Americans paid cash. War industry selected its executives and its managerial models from American companies, Canadian-domiciled or not. American troops actually occupied parts of northwestern Canada (and still separate Newfoundland) during the war. Canada benefited from the American sense, or wish, that the war was a joint enterprise and that Canadian objectives and practices were no different from American.

For the time being, links with Great Britain remained close. There was, however, a feeling that the American connection would count for more in the future.

CHAPTER SIX

Fears and Hopes,
1945–63

Canadians in 1945 did not think of the future with any special optimism. The war, they reflected, had changed things, and for the most part the change had been for the better. There were more jobs, more money, and a better life – even more food, despite rationing. All this was coming to an end, and who could say what would happen next? World War I ended with riots, strikes, and a disastrous depression. The twenties were a false dawn. The ten years' depression of the 1930s was what people remembered as normality – another dismal prospect. Public opinion polls, which had arrived in Canada in 1941, showed that what Canadians wanted above all was 'security,' meaning job and income security, and they were not sure whether their political and economic system could deliver it.

As it happened, the system did deliver. The 30 years after 1945 were the longest and most sustained period of economic growth in Canadian history. Taxes fell, incomes rose and so did standards of living, until by 1970 the Canadian standard approached the fabled and hitherto unequalled American level. Canadians grew used to full, or nearly full, employment. Because of the business structure of the period, it was stable employment – a job for life, if you chose the right (big) company, such as a bank, a department store or a big industrial concern.

These factors may have contributed to a national reputation for complacency, or in business terms, lack of imagination or enterprise. Material success, however, was not matched by spiritual comfort, for the postwar period was also a period of anxiety and, in the 1960s, dissension. 'The affluent society,' a term popularized by the émigré Canadian economist, John Kenneth Galbraith, had not produced affluent souls.

Reconstruction

Reconstruction meant the adaptation of a wartime culture to a peacetime society. At its most basic, it meant getting soldiers out of uniform and into civilian jobs. It also meant the wholesale dismantling of war regulations and war measures, and the return of life and lifestyles to civilian rhythms.

It would not be easy. Most Canadians liked what the war had done. Businessmen liked automatic markets and guaranteed prices for their products. Industrial workers liked full employment and overtime. Mothers liked family allowances, introduced in 1944 as a salary supplement by the government, payable, under the comfortable assumptions of the time, to mothers of families to use for their children, rather than to their possibly wasteful, beer-drinking husbands. What would happen, what could happen, if the government, the dispenser of good things, withdrew its hand?

Virtually the only dissenter in this climate of apprehension was the minister of reconstruction, previously the minister of munitions, C. D. Howe. Responding to a bleat from a businessman friend, who dreaded the return of an open market for (in this case) copper, Howe replied that he intended that the Canadian copper industry should be 'placed in the same position that we found them prior to the war, that is, in private business enterprise.' Howe took advantage of the fact that businessmen rhetorically were demanding a return to 'private business enterprise,' although they defined it in terms of low personal and corporate taxes that nevertheless were to pay for government subsidies and business protection.

Labour leaders took a more direct approach to the minister, surrounding him on a golf course to demand that the government-owned company they worked for continue in business (it made bomb sights and binoculars, among other things). No, Howe replied. 'The war is through, REL [the company in question] is through, and your jobs are through. Now get off the course.'

Howe believed that other jobs would be available, if not in optics, then in new technology or in consumer goods. There was 16 years of deferred demand, from the depression and the war, and the compulsory savings programmes of the war meant that hundreds of millions of dollars would shortly be released into civilian hands. War veterans received money and other benefits on discharge, plus allowances if they wished to return to school or university for training.

Mackenzie King, still prime minister, sometimes worried about Howe's penchant for saying what he meant. King had to face the electorate at the end of the war, in an election in June 1945. Instead of Howe's robust language, King promised 'full employment,' which was promptly interpreted to mean that there was a government master plan to build bridges and dig ditches all across the country. King won the election, narrowly. Canadians had put their faith, tentatively but decisively, in their dull but familiar prime minister. If stability and security were election issues, then King embodied both.

There was no master plan, but there was full employment. Tax deductions for reconversion of war industry freed up capital for investment. Investment in such things as machinery rose accordingly, up 75 per cent between 1945 and 1946. Consumer expenditure rose 15 per cent between 1944 and 1946 and another 10 per cent between 1946 and 1947. Most of this investment was domestic: there was relatively little foreign investment between 1945 and 1949.

The government did its best to restore pre-war trade patterns. It overstretched its resources and in 1946 agreed to lend $1.25 billion (equivalent to $12 billion in 2000 dollars) to Great Britain in the hope of tiding over British needs until trade had been restored. It was a vain hope. Even though the United States also lent $3.75 billion to Great Britain, it was not enough. By the middle of 1947 the British had run through their foreign-exchange reserves, and the Canadian loan was swallowed up in debt. The United States came to the rescue with the Marshall Plan in 1948, but though Canadian aid was again solicited, there was simply not enough money left for Canada to play a part.

Trade promotion through credits and loans was the government's main instrument in shoring up trade so as to provide for employment. What counted for more was pent-up savings and long-postponed demand.

Canadians believed they had to catch up. Marriage and children were things best postponed during the depression, while soldiers had little choice in the matter between 1939 and 1945. Even before the end of the war the birthrate began to creep up, and after the war there was a baby boom – *The* Baby Boom, which lasted from 1945 to 1962.

Families and babies must be housed. There was a housing shortage both during and after the war. Families coped by bribing landlords or by reducing their expectations in the hope that something better would turn up, soon. Landlords responded by building, as soon and as quickly as wartime controls on building materials could be relaxed. There was also a pronounced trend to single home ownership. New suburbs sprang up across the country, such as Don Mills in Toronto and Notre Dame de Grace (an old name for a new English-speaking development) in Montreal, with houses consisting of one bathroom, two bedrooms, living and dining rooms, and a centre hall. After a 16-year pause, normal life, or what was interpreted as normal life, had resumed.

ORGANIZING PEACE

In settling the terms of the peace following World War I, the victors hoped to prevent any such war from again breaking out. They set in place an elaborate structure of international conciliation and arbitration, and established an international body, the League of Nations, to oversee it. Failing the good will and cooperation of the great powers, and lacking the United States, the League failed, and in the 1930s the world embarked on a cycle of aggression and appeasement. Canada did little to alter the course of events, and in the opinion of many, helped undermine the League by its self-centred and isolationist policies.

World War II ended with the same good intentions among the victorious powers as at the end of World War I. To replace the League, the United Nations was created, to include all the countries that had declared war on Germany. Canada was automatically included; unlike in 1918 the Canadian government did not have to bargain for a place at the victors' table and could thus afford to take a broader perspective on the shaping of peace.

Canadians had meanwhile reinterpreted the experience of the 1930s. It was seen, in the words of a later commentator, as 'a low, dishonest decade,' in which the democracies had cravenly bargained away their strength for the sake of a temporary peace. Confrontation with the dictators, like Hitler, would have been the better policy, and it was a mistake that must not be repeated.

At least there was an international organization, the United Nations. Yet the UN, like the League, had its inescapable flaws. None of the great powers, and especially the Americans and the Soviets, would join a body where they could not wield a veto. The Americans and the Soviets got their veto, and the British, French and Chinese besides. If these powers all agreed, then the UN could prescribe for world security. If not . . . The Canadians settled for an amendment to the UN founding document, the Charter, which stipulated that smaller powers would not have to contribute to UN security operations unless they consented first – in other words, that the smaller powers, including Canada, would not be the automatic playthings of the great.

The most important question to confront the UN was atomic weapons. The bomb that had ended a war was the first weapon that could destroy the world. Canada was one of the three nations that had built the first atomic bombs that had ended the war with Japan, and when the UN organized a special commission to consider what to do with atomic bombs, Canada was one of the members.

The commission could not agree what to do. The Soviet Union, secretly rushing to achieve its own atomic bomb, demanded that the Americans surrender theirs. The Americans, prudently enough, demanded stringent international controls. The Canadians, who could not resolve the large questions by themselves, concentrated on technical details in the hope that an agreement founded on cooperation in small things could eventually produce confidence in larger matters. Mutual trust was indeed the crux of the matter, but more than a year of fruitless and increasingly recriminatory debate diminished rather than augmented that quality.

Disagreements in the atomic energy commission were mirrored in the UN General Assembly and the Security Council. The veto ensured that the UN would not or could not work, and on large matters the UN remained paralyzed for the next 40 years. The powers were left to work out their relations outside the UN, according to more traditional methods. Those methods and Canadian diplomacy, depended very much on the nature of the powers concerned.

The Cold War

At the end of the war, western leaders were notably ill informed about what kind of country the Soviet Union, their wartime ally, might be. The Soviet Union, Mackenzie King's ambassador to Moscow reported, was a very different society from the democracy that King was used to. Under the form of a people's dictatorship it was, in fact, a repressive oligarchy that sought, above all, to preserve the oligarchs' power and status.

This was not precisely news that Mackenzie King wanted to hear. His domestic agenda was full with reconversion, and with an elaborate social security scheme his advisers had developed for presentation to the provinces. Instead, in September 1945, King learned that Igor Gouzenko, a cypher clerk at the Soviet embassy, had arrived on the doorstep of the minister of justice with a sheaf of documents that he claimed proved the existence of two Soviet spy rings in Canada.

King had no idea what to do. Gouzenko was turned away – it was, after all, a weekend – as the prime minister considered his dilemma. If he gave asylum to Gouzenko, he might offend the Soviet Union and make Canada the place and the cause for a major rift among the great powers. On the other hand, Gouzenko might be right. When the desperate would-be defector threatened to commit suicide, King grasped at the opportunity: in that case, he told the police, they should seize the Soviet documents. But finally King could hold out no longer: the documents *and* Gouzenko were taken into custody. The documents proved to be genuine and, eventually, a score of suspects were arrested, and some were later convicted, including Canada's only communist member of parliament. Already distrustful of communism and communists, most Canadians were not surprised.

Western relations with the Soviet Union proceeded straight downhill. The Soviets extended not only their influence but also their system of government across the East European countries they occupied in 1945. A communist coup in Czechoslovakia in February 1948 climaxed the process and stimulated the British to call for a western alliance to resist further communist expansion. Discussions in

Washington later in 1948 laid the foundations for a North Atlantic Treaty, duly signed in the same city in April 1949.

Canada participated fully in the North Atlantic negotiations, arguing for a strong and multi-faceted alliance that would include more than political guarantees or military assistance. The Canadian foreign minister, Lester B. Pearson, and a new prime minister, King's successor, Louis St. Laurent, wanted an instrument to resist communism, but they also wished for a partnership between Canada and Europe that would vary Canadian reliance on the overwhelming neighbour, the United States. What they got was a political alliance (the North Atlantic Treaty Organization – NATO) that guaranteed that Canada and the United States would come to the aid of any alliance member attacked by the Soviet Union. The signatories in Washington hoped that the promise would be enough. They proved to be wrong.

THE 1950s

The 1950s began with a literal bang – the explosion of a Soviet atomic bomb in September 1949. It was the first of many shocks. The next month, a communist government was proclaimed in Beijing, and the world's most populous nation aligned itself with the communist bloc. In June 1950, communist North Korea invaded noncommunist South Korea.

Led by the United States, the United Nations sent an army to Korea, which shortly found itself embroiled with 'volunteers' sent by the Beijing government. The Korean War would last just over three years, producing over one million dead (including 312 Canadians) and costing billions of dollars; but for Canada, the Korean War was not the main event. Fearing a wider Soviet attack, Canada began a serious rearmament programme and doubled the size of its armed forces. An army brigade was sent to Korea, and another to Germany, along with an air division of 12 squadrons, to serve with NATO. Defence spending moved from 16 per cent of the federal budget in 1950 to 45 per cent in 1953.

The Atomic Age

Canadians were used to sending troops abroad: wars had been some-thing that occurred elsewhere, because of the thousands of miles that lay between North America and any conceivable enemy. The 1950s were the first decade when enemy airpower could reach North America, and air attack also meant atomic attack. Canadian airspace suddenly became valuable, for Canada was the likely highway for bombers, incoming and outgoing. Eventually three radar fences snaked across Canadian territory: the Pinetree Line, along the 49th parallel, the Mid-Canada Line, at the 55th, and the Distant Early Warning (DEW) Line along the Arctic Coast. The cost was formidable – in the billions by the time the DEW Line was built, requiring a contribution by the United States. These warning systems would, it was hoped, give decision makers in Washington and Ottawa a couple of hours to decide what to do if the Soviet Union decided to send over its bombers.

Canadian troops and airmen in Europe also entered the atomic age when NATO decided that Europe could only be defended by atomic weapons – small, tactical ones, unlike the increasingly massive airborne bombs. The Canadian air division (20 per cent of NATO's airpower) in 1954 received a strike-reconnaissance mission. In the event of a Soviet attack on Western Europe, Allied air forces had the task of dropping atomic weapons on Soviet supply lines and troop concentrations moving through Poland and Czechoslovakia to the front line in Ger-many. Canadian pilots, like other Allied airmen, got a small piece of extra equipment – an eyepatch to shield one of their eyes from the atomic blast.

There was almost no dissent at home about Canada's commitment to the western side in the Cold War, or about Canada's role in Europe. Canadians took pride in their close relations with the United States and Great Britain although, like the British in this period, they had difficulty coming to grips with what lay beyond the English Channel.

Canadian attitudes toward Great Britain in the 1950s were a com-bination of popular affection and official ambivalence. The wartime experience, the war brides and then massive immigration from the British Isles after the war gave postwar Canada a British tinge. Royal weddings, funerals and coronations were followed with rapt attention and the occasional royal tours attracted crowds in the many thousands.

Canadian officials and the Canadian educated elite generally (foreign minister Pearson was but one example among many) were often educated in Great Britain and had both more experience of and more affection for 'the old country' than for the American cousins just south of the border. The trouble was that the 'old country' was far less important in the postwar world than the United States. Great Britain could no longer afford to buy much that Canada produced, and the United States had both the money to invest in Canada and to buy Canadian goods. Neither Britain nor Canada could do without the United States, and even Anglo-Canadian relations had to be conducted in the shadow of American power.

This fact became painfully obvious in 1956 when, in a last gasp of old-style, gunboat imperialism, Great Britain and France attempted to repossess the Suez Canal, previously the property of their investors, from Egypt, which had seized it. The Canadian government disapproved, and prime minister Louis St Laurent disapproved in particular. The day of 'the supermen of Europe' was over, St Laurent told Parliament, and Canada could not support a foolish enterprise like the Anglo-French Suez expedition. Instead, Pearson piloted through the United Nations a resolution replacing the Anglo-French troops (and the Israelis, who had joined the war) with a UN force. It was a measure strongly supported by the United States, which had chosen not to back its European allies in this post-colonial adventure.

Pearson designed his UN force as a face-saving measure for the British, and he knew well enough that many in the British foreign office and military both disapproved what their government was doing and approved Pearson's solution. The next year, Pearson won the Nobel Prize for peace for his accomplishment. Ironically, the Canadian public was much less enthusiastic than the Nobel prize committee, and had already voted Pearson and the Liberals out of office. It was a last spasm of Canadian affection for the British Empire; but it was also a barometer of Canadian feelings about the United States. Canadian nationalism was about to take an anti-American direction.

American Influence on Canada

'It's getting so I feel like staying away from the club,' a Calgary matron confided to a friend in 1957. 'There are so many Americans there.' The worst thing, she added, was their unfailing sense of cheery hospitality: 'They're forever trying to make me feel at home in my own club.'

Other Canadians had much the same feeling. In Toronto, a Liberal (and highly successful) businessman, Walter Gordon, began a campaign to persuade the Canadian government, and other Canadians, that massive American investment in Canada was denaturing the Canadian business class, in effect, robbing Canada of its ability to be different.

Certainly Canada was not as different as some Canadians would have preferred it to be. Nor had it ever been. American ideas, American magazines, American music, American money had always freely crossed the border, and every summer floods of Americans came, to enjoy Canadian woods and lakes, and to pour American dollars into happy Canadian tourist resorts. It was, on the whole, a beneficent exchange, but it was not an equal one: there were ten times as many Americans as Canadians, and their presence, as the Calgary matron discovered, could be overwhelming.

The songs of Stephen Foster were popular in Canada in the 1850s, as were, later, the songs of Irving Berlin in the 1910s and Cole Porter in the 1930s. In fact, Canadian music was indistinguishable from the American product, and can be said to have contributed to it: Guy Lombardo and his band 'the Royal Canadians' serenaded Americans every New Year's from New York's Roosevelt Grill – an American institution. Paul Anka, an Ottawa boy, found success, fame and fortune on American pop charts. If Americans ever knew, or reflected on the fact that these were Canadians, it served to underline that Americans and Canadians were, after all, just the same. When Elvis Presley, the rock and roll phenomenon of the 1950s, thanked an Ottawa audience for the 50,000 Christmas cards he had got from Canada, Canadian traditionalists winced: this was not their idea of Canada. But then it wasn't American traditionalists' view of the United States either.

Canada's highly traditionalist and very nationalist governor general in the 1950s, Vincent Massey, did his best to combat American incursions. He might have included his film star brother Raymond in the prohibited list. Raymond made a living impersonating Abe Lincoln and other American figures to the satisfaction of American audiences, and incidentally considered his brother insufferably pompous.

'We can never equal the United States in terms of size,' Vincent admitted. 'It will always build higher buildings; it will always have larger crowds. American life has pace and magnitude and glamour. It has immense vitality and exuberance too, but these things must not blind us to the quality of our own life...' Canadians in the 1950s and for years before had indeed not been blind to the quality of their own life: they measured it constantly and anxiously against American life and if the difference were too great, they emigrated. (One computation in the 1990s showed that eight American Nobel prize winners in science were in fact born in Canada: they, or their parents, had followed opportunity south; Lester Pearson's brother left for Boston, and prime minister St Laurent's grandson fetched up as a sheriff in Florida.)

Canadian life in the years after 1945 closely followed American patterns and styles. Canadian suburbs were not much different from

Post-war growth: a polymer artificial rubber factory in Ontario

American – though they were smaller than the biggest American postwar developments. Canadian public and office buildings reached toward the sky, as in the United States, only not as high. American movies appealed to Canadian audiences, as did American radio and television. Canadians ate American cereal (possibly produced in Canada), discovered backyard barbecues after a slight time lag, and kept their meat and milk in American-designed and -sized refrigerators. Especially in the 1950s, the differences between North American styles and standards of living and those of Europe were wide and, to North Americans, gratifying.

Nor were there strong differences in opinions, as measured in public opinion polls. According to a sociological study in the 1990s, Canadians and Americans agreed over time on about 85 per cent of items compared by pollsters, more than any other two countries. 'The narcissism of small differences,' sniffed an American historian, in considering the views of Canadians such as Vincent Massey on the United States.

The 'small differences' came to the fore in a political debate in 1956. It was originally a scheme by C. D. Howe to bring Canadian natural gas from Alberta to Ontario, thereby avoiding dependence on the United States for central Canadian energy supply. Howe wanted his project, organized a company to build it with government aid, and he wanted it to start in 1956. The parliamentary opposition, on the other hand, wanted to portray Howe and the Liberal government as dictatorial. All they needed to do was delay the bill authorizing his project in the House of Commons, and this they did. The government then rammed the bill through using closure – a parliamentary device cutting off debate. The bill went through, the pipeline would be built, and the government lost a tremendous battle in public opinion and, eventually, the next election.

A large part of the debate surrounding the pipeline concerned the company that would build it. It was American. Howe, the opposition reminded Canadians, had been born in the United States. It was a sign that Howe and the government in which he served were slavishly pro-American, or so it was claimed. Then, the same year, Pearson helped the Americans over Suez and abandoned the British. It was too much. Boasting that they would restore links with the British and with

Canada's past, the opposition Conservatives defeated Prime Minister St Laurent in a general election in June 1957 – the first election the federal Liberals had lost in 22 years.

A NEW CANADIAN IDENTITY

The Cold War stressed the similarities between Canadians and Americans while highlighting certain differences in approach, which help clarify the (slightly) differing political cultures and political situations of the two countries. Canadians remained 'on side' during the whole of the Cold War, but their government was, more than the American, prone to explore any possible avenue for hope, for a thaw in the international glacier that passed for diplomacy in the 1950s. Yet of course the Canadians could afford to explore: they were not imprisoned, like the Americans, in a network of alliances that forced a constant balancing of the views of allies from Turkey to Australia. The Canadian government's task was simpler: it balanced itself mostly in the context of the United States and Western Europe.

Canadians emphasized their differing approaches – they contributed to a self-image that was an extension of Vincent Massey's depiction of Canadians as smaller in scope, more restrained and less excitable: more *moderate*, smaller but *useful*. Eventually, Pearson's diplomatic skill in achieving a peacekeeping force and his ability to exploit the media, the quality that made him unique and indispensable in 1956, would be forgotten, while the message he brought, peacekeeping, would be remembered – a quality which, it was assumed, made Canadians unique and indispensable.

John Diefenbaker, the Conservative leader who became prime minister in 1957, was believed by his followers to embody a new, self-confident Canadian identity. Diefenbaker was certainly a man of considerable parts. Imposing, intelligent and a brilliant speaker and debater, he was also mistrustful of his followers, resentful of the Canadian elite, and hasty in his judgement of personalities, issues and events. His talents catapulted him into power unexpectedly, and his defects eventually drove him out of office in 1963.

Diefenbaker had his share of misfortune, which characteristically he failed to understand and preferred to blame on others. Unemployment

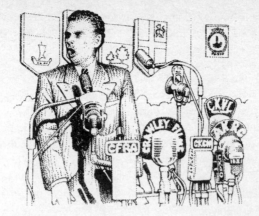

John Diefenbaker, the Conservative leader in the 1958 election

rose in 1957, and remained high until 1961. Diefenbaker at first blamed the Liberals and then practised and preached denial, only to discover that when the unemployment figures finally fell, nobody believed them, or him. His time in office coincided with a reluctant British decision to join the recently founded European Common Market, the ancestor of the European Union. This affected Canadian exports to Great Britain, which would no longer receive favourable duties and would, in fact, be excluded by the Common Market's protectionist agricultural policies. But Diefenbaker had refused to consider negotiating a free trade agreement with the British when they had proposed it, in 1957, and the British government took his later, vociferous objections to their Common Market decision badly. Anglo-Canadian relations, far from improving under the Conservative Diefenbaker, fell to an all-time low.

Diefenbaker, incredibly, went one step further by quarrelling with the Americans. Although Diefenbaker was by no means personally anti-American (he liked US president Eisenhower, in office 1953–61, and went out of his way to oblige him) he distrusted the much younger successor, John F. Kennedy. Diefenbaker saw Kennedy as a spoiled rich man's son and failed to keep his opinion to himself. Diefenbaker was also conscious that Kennedy was admired in Canada as stylish and eloquent and might even be more popular than he was on his home turf. Nothing was better guaranteed to arouse Diefenbaker's considerable store of bile.

The Diefenbaker government, without really intending it, fell into a dispute with the Kennedy administration over the storage and use of American nuclear weapons by Canadian forces. Endless delay resulted, in the midst of which, in October 1962, Kennedy had to face a crisis brought on by the emplacement of Soviet nuclear missiles in newly communist Cuba. Diefenbaker proved a grudging ally on this occasion, further irritating Kennedy and his entourage. If it had only been Kennedy, Diefenbaker's troubles might not have been too serious. Unfortunately for him, Canadian public opinion supported Kennedy's boldness in facing down the Soviet challenge, and in forcing the removal of the missiles in Cuba, rather than Diefenbaker's all too public hesitation.

Diefenbaker's own ministers disagreed about what to do next, while the prime minister, unable to decide on a course of action – whether or not to take nuclear warheads for equipment already bought and in use by Canadian troops – dithered. His cabinet fell around his ears, the government was defeated on a confidence vote in the House of Commons, and Diefenbaker was defeated in a general election in April 1963.

It was an inglorious finish to a government that had begun with the promise of renewing Canada's sense of purpose, adrift as the British Empire disappeared over the horizon, and redefining Canadians' sense of themselves. It was left to Lester Pearson, as leader of the Liberal opposition and Diefenbaker's successor as prime minister, to find what had eluded the Conservatives.

CHAPTER SEVEN

The Transformation of Quebec, 1920–80

The history of Canada includes the history of Quebec, and the history of Quebec likewise is inseparable from that of Canada; and yet the two histories take different tangents. This was especially the case in the last half of the twentieth century, a period when Quebec was more similar to the rest of Canada than ever before but nevertheless veered toward political separation from the rest of the country.

Landscape and Language

There are in fact two Quebecs, French and English speaking, just as there are two Canadas. English Quebec before 1950 was the western part of Montreal and Montreal Island, and a few rural pockets east (the Eastern Townships), northwest and south of the metropolis. Except for Montreal and the area immediately around Ottawa, English Quebec had been losing population for decades – since at least the 1880s. While the English population around Montreal grew steadily, thanks to immigration, people tended to move out of the city proper and into suburbs to the west and north.

Physically, English Montreal resembled the other large cities of North America, ranging from the lofty heights of Westmount, through the elegant apartment buildings of Sherbrooke Street, to the slums of Point St Charles. Convenient commuter trains brought in office workers and executives from Beaconsfield or Baie d'Urfé or Town of Mount Royal (TMR). The city centred on its mountain, Mont Royal or Mount Royal, conveniently landscaped and turned into a magnificent park, 'a work of art' in the 1880s by the great American landscape

Château Frontenac, Quebec City

architect, Frederick Law Olmstead, the designer of Central Park in
New York. The suburbs were not all English. The French bourgeoisie
preferred Outremont, like Westmount situated on the slopes of the
mountain, and the French quarter of the city descended, like the
English, until it reached its riverside slums.

French Quebec only became predominantly urban around 1940,
when the war drew farm boys and girls into factories producing tanks,
aircraft, textiles and chemicals that dotted Montreal and the cities of the
plain around it. French Quebec had been a favourite study for
sociologists attracted by its apparent lack of change – the villages along
the St Lawrence each topped by the metal spire of the large parish
church, ringed by the steep tin roofs of the parishioners' houses, which
were built of wood or stone from the early days, brick or the cheaper
Insulbrick later on. In Quebec alone in North America, wine flowed
through the age of temperance and prohibition. And from 1920 to 1940,
Quebec alone in North America refused to give women the vote, a
measure only brought in by a reforming provincial Liberal government
during the war; the women used it in the next provincial election to help
defeat the Liberals and return a traditionalist nationalist government.

The Quebec provincial government of Maurice Duplessis (1944–59)
appealed to economic conservatism and a desire for social stability. The
economic conservatism kept the English businessmen of Montreal
happy, for it included a traditional allotment of timber rights on provincial lands, and a cooperative attitude toward the mines and hydro-
electric companies that played a large part in the provincial economy.
Duplessis broke with tradition in appointing a French Canadian his
finance minister. Up to that point, every single minister of finance in

Quebec had been an English Canadian, an outward symbol of the marriage of interest and fact between Montreal money and Quebec politics. In fact that made little difference to the way business was conducted. The premier expected his friends to receive appropriate legal work (and fees) and to have his achievements recognized by contributions at election time.

It has always been good politics to blame somebody else, and federal systems are well adapted to political scapegoating. The practice has been raised to an art in Canada where provincial governments more often than not blame Ottawa for deficiencies real and imagined. For Duplessis, it was easy and electorally profitable to blame 'les autres' – the English majority in Canada – and to claim that the government in Quebec responded only to 'nous-mêmes' – ourselves. To emphasize this fact, as he claimed it to be, Duplessis in 1948 proclaimed a provincial flag, based on an eighteenth-century French design.

Duplessis placed great store in Quebec's unique education and welfare systems, religiously divided, and divided too by language. The Roman Catholic Church administered school systems for both French and English Catholics, and managed its own welfare establishment as well. The crucifix hung in classrooms, hospital rooms and the provincial legislature, appropriately enough for a province where 85 per cent of the population was Roman Catholic, and church-going Roman Catholic at that. The swish of the soutane and the crocodile lines of nuns' habits were daily sounds and sights in Quebec – where, in 1951, members of religious orders numbered 45,000 in a population of 4 million.

This was the Quebec that traditionalists liked to imagine, and it was the Quebec that English Canadians believed would never change. Canada was stable because Quebec was stable, for behind the line of fulminating politicians – Duplessis and his ilk – a kneeling army of priests occupied the province. The image was true enough, as far as it went, which was not, in fact, very far.

THE WIND OF CHANGE

Statistics tell a different story from the vision of *un Québec touristique*. More and more French Canadians lived in cities and in particular in the one big city, Montreal. They lived better in the cities than their parents and relatives did in the country – the common history of virtually every migration from rural to urban life. Arriving in the city, they found that business was urban. Montreal's downtown, its shopping areas, were strictly segregated by language. French Canadians, if they wished to be served in their own language, went to Dupuis Frères at the east end of downtown. In the west end, exemplified by Eaton's, Simpson's and Ogilvy's, clerks and customers spoke English. Many of the clerks and many of the customers were French Canadian, but that made no difference. The language 'downtown,' and of course further west in the English suburbs, was English. That had not been as noticeable in the countryside, where in mixed areas bilingualism was common, and where the English enclaves were so geographically isolated the issue did not often arise. It was very clear in the city.

The dominance of English downtown, in offices and in retail and in Montreal's most prominent university, the English language McGill, suggested to Quebec nationalists that French was under threat. If the majority language was not spoken, it was surely the result of discrimination, they argued. French Canadians were an oppressed majority; English Quebeckers were behaving like 'Rhodesians,' the minority whites in present-day Zimbabwe, who were trying to preserve their rule over a black majority deprived of civil rights. There was, however, one difference: French Canadians had the right to vote, and the government of the province was one that they chose. Things could change, clearly enough.

Clear too was the fact that in the Montreal of the 1950s French Canadians were at the bottom of the economic ladder as statisticians measure these things – by income. They made less than the English Canadians did, but they also made less than the immigrants did, including immigrants just off the boat. Of course there were rich and privileged French Canadians, and many of them, but for those who noticed such things, there was the uncomfortable realization that in the province where they were a majority French Canadians were at a disadvantage.

The 1950s were boom years in Quebec, as elsewhere in the country. In Montreal, the Canadian National Railway, the federal railway company, built a state-of-the-art new hotel, proudly named after Canada's monarch, Elizabeth II. Protests that the name should have more local significance – named after Montreal's French founder, for example, were ignored. Across the street from the hotel, Canada's first postwar skyscraper complex, Place Ville-Marie – PVM to the English – was rising, a clear indication of Montreal's prosperity and its determination to remain Canada's premier metropolis, ahead of upstart Toronto, where comparable projects were still in the dreaming stage.

More and more Canadians, and more and more Canadians in Quebec too, were finishing high school, attending university, and attending graduate schools, at home, or in England, the United States and even France. A highly educated elite was not so much created as significantly reinforced in this period, and by the 1950s it was in a position to challenge what had traditionally been in place.

Behind the suburban wall and the glittering office towers, Quebec's institutions in the 1950s were in a state of crisis. The Catholic Church, the institutional foundation for education and welfare, was cracking under the strain of providing services for the millions of Quebeckers who now lived in cities. Money was the first issue, and to the church Premier Duplessis doled out subsidies, and by the 1950s very large subsidies. Without these infusions of cash, the leaders of the church knew, they could not sustain their role. Duplessis was widely quoted (accurately or not) as saying 'The bishops eat out of my hand.' While this was an exaggeration, it had many grains of uncomfortable truth at its core.

THE QUIET REVOLUTION

In September 1959 Premier Duplessis died. Within months, his system crumbled and his conservative-nationalist party, the Union Nationale, was swept out of office in a provincial election in June 1960. The Liberals, who won the election, promised reform, which was generally taken to mean a reform of the electoral system and an end to some of the more egregious forms of political patronage. Quebec, commentators assumed, would become more like other Canadian provinces and would enter, finally, the progressive end of the twentieth century.

The new premier, Jean Lesage, was a veteran of the federal Liberal party and had served as a federal cabinet minister. Again it was assumed that this would bind both Lesage and Quebec more firmly to the Canadian norm, which was true up to a point. Lesage had seen what government was doing in Ottawa, and had imbibed the notion that government could and should do more, much more, to direct society. He shared too the view of the liberal-minded in the 1950s and 1960s that government could and should expand the welfare system. But, and it was a very important qualification, Lesage had also had the experience of being a minority man in a majority system, in Ottawa, where the language of the bureaucracy, of parliament and of cabinet was English. Though Lesage was and remained throughout his life 'a good Canadian,' as he saw it, that did not preclude bringing Quebec up to a modern standard in its own way and within its own jurisdiction.

Lesage discovered that he had a fund of talent to draw upon – French Canadians with degrees from Stanford or Harvard or Oxford or the London School of Economics – who were anxious to work in a good cause. He attracted as well French Canadians, equally well qualified, with experience in federal institutions. Less under Lesage's direction than under his authority, these newly minted Quebec civil servants set to work to expand and exploit the role of government, and in particular of the province of Quebec.

Within a very few years, by 1966, Quebec had a new pension plan, a provincial investment fund, and a provincially owned hydro-electric utility (the last province to have one). Plans were afoot for a Quebec steel plant, on the grounds that no truly modern society could be without its own steel industry. Canada already had a steel industry, but it was in Ontario. It was a sign that the directing civil servants and some of their political masters in Quebec were no longer thinking in Canadian terms, or had very quickly come to the conclusion that Canada's interests and Quebec's were not necessarily the same.

Lesage initially sought to claim what Quebec was owed under the existing Canadian constitution. Provincial rights and responsibilities, for Quebec as for all provinces, were very broad. Paradoxically, because the constitutional framers of 1867 expected the federal authority to have the most important tasks of government, they gave Ottawa most of the revenue. Ottawa in turn used its superior financial position, not to mention the very weak economic situation of most of the provinces, to bribe (more correctly to 'induce') provincial governments into conformity with federal plans and directions. This was 'fiscal federalism.'

Lesage, proposing to strike out on his own, wanted no direction from Ottawa, but he did want its money. He had the advantage that his fellow Liberal and former cabinet colleague, Lester Pearson, was in power in Ottawa after 1963. Better still, Pearson was seriously alarmed by the upsurge in nationalist Quebec feeling in the 1960s, and he was prepared to appease that feeling. As a result, Quebec acquired its own pension plan while Canada had another, parallel plan. Pearson gave the provinces more fiscal room and might have been prepared to give more. On one occasion, while Pearson held a meeting with all ten provincial premiers in Quebec City, he was uncomfortably aware that students were rioting outside.

While Lesage and Pearson dickered and bickered, larger changes were afoot. Lesage created a department of education to supervise the province's school system, ending the century-old supremacy of the church. In effect, Lesage, without entirely understanding the event, was ratifying what had already happened. The church could no longer manage by itself: state aid must now be supplemented by state direction.

For the church, it became necessary to adjust to a smaller role in Quebec society. Recruiting for the priesthood and various religious orders shrank. The lights gradually went out in the convents scattered around the province. In downtown Montreal, the new, secular Université de Québec placed its entrance hall inside the shell of a church, the perfect expression of the change that was overcoming the province.

THE INDEPENDENCE MOVEMENT

And would Quebec be a province for much longer? There had always existed a tiny fringe that claimed independence as Quebec's destiny. Some intellectuals dreamed that someday a French-speaking republic could be erected on the banks of the St Lawrence, but their aspirations were confined to obscure novels and fringe periodicals. French Canadian nationalists accepted a limited identification with Canada even if, like Duplessis, they were suspicious of an active and enter-prising federal government's encroachments on the traditional forms and institutions of Quebec society.

In the late 1950s a few fringe political groups demanding indepen-dence (usually called 'separation' and believers were called 'separatists') appeared, with no electoral effect. By 1962, rallies were being held and what had been unspeakable and unthinkable in polite society was merely undesirable, unless English Canada proved to be immovable and obdurate in the face of Quebec's newly discovered needs. Words translated into actions in early 1963: a bomb was discovered on the route of Prime Minister Diefenbaker's campaign train. From 1963 until 1970 life in Quebec featured low-key terrorism: bombs in postboxes, in armouries, and once in the Montreal stock exchange. If the politi-cians could not work things out, the bombs seemed to suggest, there were others waiting in the wings. The range of political debate moved from a contest between nationalists supporting more autonomy for Quebec and Liberals with greater or lesser connections to Ottawa, to a struggle between federalists of all stripes and 'separatists.'

Pearson realized that French Canadians' sense of representation in Ottawa was perilously weak. He first tried to accommodate traditional grievances by modifying the unilingually English character of the federal government. French Canadians were consciously recruited for the civil service and for the Liberal Party. The government then sent senior civil servants back to school to learn French, and more junior ranks learned that serious promotion could only come after a desire to learn French had been manifested. On the political side, for the 1965 federal election, Pearson recruited three prominent French Canadian supporters of federalism: Jean Marchand, a labour leader, Gérard Pel-letier, a prominent editor, and Pierre Elliott Trudeau, a law professor and professional intellectual. Trudeau was considered the least important of the three, and was thought so unelectable that the Liberals found him a constituency that was overwhelmingly English speaking. None of the three wished to see any major redistribution of powers within the Canadian constitution: all three argued that Quebec under existing rules had as much jurisdiction as it could conceivably need.

Within a year, Pelletier and Marchand had been eclipsed by

Trudeau, whose intelligence, flair and ostentatious nonconformity caught public attention. Trudeau wore an ascot tie to the House of Commons (not seen there since the nineteenth century) and drove his Mercedes convertible down Ottawa's dull and leafy streets. There had not been a truly colourful figure in Canadian politics in many years – perhaps not since Sir Wilfrid Laurier and his white plume in the 1900s. Trudeau became minister of justice, and as such took charge of the federal government's constitutional strategy.

This political change in Ottawa overlapped with a political change in Quebec. Many Quebeckers objected to the pace of change, or to change at all. In the 1966 provincial election their sentiments prevailed. Lesage and the Liberals lost to the old nationalist opposition, under a veteran politician, Daniel Johnson (despite the name, a French speaker). Johnson neither reversed nor significantly slowed the revolution in Quebec's institutions: change was by 1966 something that politicians could at best channel but not reverse. Johnson instead tried to make his mark on the Canadian constitution. It must change, he proclaimed. He promised that he would seek 'equality or independence,' evidently meaning that if Quebec were to stay in Canada it would have to achieve equality with the rest of the country in Canada's constitutional structures. This was a difficult proposition, given that Quebec had a mere 28 per cent of the country's population, and Johnson was wise enough not to push it.

Instead, he settled back to see which way the wind blew, a sensible course for a leader who understood that his potential following was deeply uncertain. 'What does Quebec want?' English Canadians of the period liked to ask. The answer was that Quebec did not know; no more did Johnson.

De Gaulle, Trudeau and Quebec

In 1967 Canada celebrated its centennial. The centrepiece was a world exposition in Montreal, called Expo '67. To mark the anniversary, Canada invited the leaders of the world to come to its shores, with a trip to Expo '67 thrown in. Everyone came, from Elizabeth II to President Lyndon B. Johnson of the United States. And of course President

Charles de Gaulle on his historic visit to Canada in 1967 which gave heart to French-speaking separatists

Charles de Gaulle of France was invited too. When de Gaulle finally let it be known that he would come, he made it clear that he would do his best to ignore the federal government whose anniversary he was supposed to be feting, and would pay assiduous attention to the provincial government of Quebec. In a climactic speech, capping his visit, he saluted Quebec and more: 'Vive le Québec libre!' de Gaulle shouted, repeating a well-known separatist slogan.

It was an unusual action by the leader of a country that was, officially and unofficially, an ally of Canada in two world wars and in NATO. Though de Gaulle had a clear political effect, he was ultimately speaking from weakness. The French empire of his youth had disintegrated, France had lost its North African colonies, and the place in the world of France and the French language was declining. France's leadership had been taken over by the British and then the Americans. English had replaced French, even in Europe. The largest group of French speakers in the world, outside of France, was Quebec. Yet Quebec too was threatened and de Gaulle meant to make a difference to its fate.

De Gaulle's speech was immediately repudiated by the federal government and the French leader promptly and happily left Canada. In Paris his cabinet gathered at the airport to greet him, anxiously studying their president for any evident signs of dementia. In Ottawa justice minister Trudeau, getting into his convertible after an emergency cabinet meeting, shouted derisively, 'Vive la Bretagne libre!' France too had its minorities, he told the press.

As he intended, de Gaulle's visit was a catalyst for further events. The provincial Liberal Party split on the question of 'separatism,' with one faction under René Lévesque that preferred a soft version of independence going one way, and the majority under Lesage opting for continuing membership in the Canadian federation.

Lévesque, a charismatic personality, trained as a radio and television journalist, may have been the most attractive political figure of his day, at least in Quebec. His shrug, his rumpled clothes, his downturned mouth with a cigarette dangling from it, evoked 'the little guy,' a Chaplinesque image that reminded French Canadians of themselves, of what they were. It was a complete contrast with the steely Trudeau whose elegance and strident eloquence, some said, reminded Quebeckers of what they might be – or might have been. No-one could argue that Trudeau had the common touch, but there was something admirable about him.

Lévesque founded his own political party, which he eventually labelled the Parti Québécois or PQ. It stood for 'sovereignty-association,' meaning independence plus a common market and perhaps other good economic things with English Canada. Quebeckers could have independence and all the psychological good that brought, could cease to be a minority, could at last make their basic decisions in French and not have to negotiate them with the English. At the same time they could preserve their standard of living and, in 'association' with the English, have 'equality.' It would be the end of English majority rule, Canadian-style.

De Gaulle naturally approved. Federations of different language groups were unnatural, he told a press conference in Paris. Just look at Cyprus: civil war. Nigeria was the same. And Canada? Another British creation! The only problem, a difficult one for a man who saw the world in classically political terms and not economic, was that there was no money to back up his vision. The French state was having an economic crisis. French business mulishly preferred to invest in English Canada, if was to invest in Canada at all. And

Daniel Johnson, the Quebec premier, proved to be an unworthy partner.

Quebec's French-speaking business elite told the premier that Quebec's economic situation did not allow for independence. Opportunist by temperament and conviction, Johnson veered back to Canada, and left de Gaulle's shining words behind. In a debate with Trudeau at a federal-provincial conference early in 1968, the premier was crushed. Trudeau went on to become national Liberal leader and prime minister, in April 1968, called a federal election in June, won a majority, and he prepared to confront Johnson that autumn from a position of strength.

Johnson, however, was no longer there. Afflicted by a heart condition, he died in November 1968. The provincial Liberals, under a new, young leader, Robert Bourassa, defeated his successor in April 1970. Trudeau could afford to be optimistic.

THE OCTOBER CRISIS AND THE CRISIS OF FEDERALISM

The 1970 provincial election did more than return the Liberals, a federalist party, to power. It undermined the old nationalist party that had been the vehicle for Duplessis and Johnson; instead, second in the popular vote was Lévesque's new Parti Québécois (PQ). In the next election, 1973, the PQ not only came second in terms of vote, but in seats. In a political system where parties alternate in power, the alternative was now separatist.

The electoral emergence of the PQ coincided with another eruption of political terrorism. In October 1970, a group of terrorists kidnapped the British trade commissioner (consul) in Montreal. In return for his release they demanded the liberation of a number of 'political prisoners' (terrorists) who had been condemned for a series of bombings and the occasional murder over the previous seven years. They wanted their revolutionary manifesto (among other things, it attacked Bourassa as a homosexual, which he happened not to be) read over the airwaves. They also wanted money or gold, and safe passage to a friendly country.

The provincial and federal governments declined these terms, and so the terrorists struck again, kidnapping Quebec's minister of labour, Pierre Laporte. This time the authorities were shaken, and some, like

Bourassa, panicked. The Quebec provincial government begged Trudeau to send in the army to reinforce the police, and to proclaim federal emergency legislation dating from World War I. Trudeau did as he was asked; he and his colleagues in Ottawa had come to believe that the Quebec provincial government might crumble if they did not. There were rumours that it might be replaced by a government inclined to compromise with the terrorists, or even to compromise Quebec's standing within Canada.

The dispatch of the army and a police round up of 'suspects' (some reasonable, some not) did not save the luckless minister of labour, who was murdered by his kidnappers. They were eventually caught, condemned by the courts, and sent to jail. Eventually, in December 1970, the British trade commissioner was found and released, in return for free passage to Cuba for his captors. The suspects were released, and after a few months Quebec and Canada returned to normal.

The October Crisis of 1970 was the single most serious political challenge to the Canadian state since 1867 or even 1837. Yet it was more revolutionary drama than incendiary insurrection. The number of terrorists involved was minuscule: including their immediate followers or dupes it was probably no more than 100. The federal government met drama with drama – armed soldiers, emergency legislation, midnight arrests, an icy television address by a prime minister standing up for order and democracy. In effect, the government terrorized the terrorists, and it worked. Acts of revolutionary violence subsided, terrorists found other lines of work, and the world returned to normal.

It is hard to escape the conclusion that the October Crisis was an aberration, both on the separatist and the federalist side. Quebec (and for that matter Canada) was a democracy. A respected political leader, Lévesque, with his PQ, embodied separatist aspirations. There appeared to be a fair prospect that separatism would succeed without violating the rule of law, either in spirit or in fact. The federalist crackdown on terrorists did not deeply offend most mainline separatists, and, indeed, it did nothing to diminish support for separatism in Quebec. Democracy was stronger than attempts to bypass it.

On the other hand, Trudeau caught the psychological moment, the

point at which events were beginning to move. By reasserting his
authority, using the symbols of power, he became the director of
events, rather than their servant or follower. In Canada, and in Quebec,
Trudeau and not Lévesque was the dominant leader of his generation,
and for better or worse, it would be Trudeau and not any of his rivals
whose views counted most.

THE DECLINE OF QUEBEC

The rise of separatism in Quebec coincided with a change in Quebec's
place in the Canadian economy. Over many decades but especially
since World War II, Montreal's place as Canada's economic centre had
diminished. During the 1960s, Montreal remained the headquarters for
Canada's two transcontinental railways, its largest telephone company,
its national airline and two of its largest banks. Despite these advantages, it was Toronto rather than Montreal that grew. The 'Golden
Horseshoe' of commercial and industrial communities at the head of
Lake Ontario, the concentration of finance in Toronto, the greater
proximity to the American market gave Toronto and Ontario the
edge.

　　The comparative population figures are telling. In 1951, Ontario had
4.6 million people, and Quebec 4.1 million, 500,000 apart. In 1961, it
was 6.24 million and 5.26 million, a difference of a million; and in

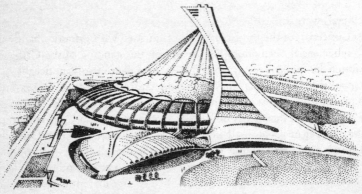

The Olympic Stadium, Quebec

1971, 7.7 million to 6.03 million, a difference of almost 1.7 million. (1997 figures, the latest available, put the difference between the provinces at 4 million.) Metropolitan Montreal, traditionally Canada's largest urban area, gave place to metropolitan Toronto around 1976, and by 1996 was a million people behind. Even the large infusions of public money that accompanied Expo '67 or the Montreal Olympics held in 1976 could not arrest the trend.

In fact, the strikes and cost overruns that accompanied the construction of the Olympic stadium, not to mention the impractical design of the stadium itself, with a retractable roof that never properly worked, did little to enhance Montreal's reputation. Labour strife reached a high in Quebec in the 1970s (it was a time of accelerating inflation). For someone like Bourassa who valued 'social peace' and feared disorder, the image of a disrupted province was a point of particular vulnerability.

There was agitation over language as well. Resentment of the superior place of English and English speakers in Quebec, and fear that French might become a folkloric relic in Quebec as it already was in Louisiana, stimulated demands for restrictions on English. The Bourassa government obliged, with an act requiring the use of French in some workplaces, and, on public signs, obligatory equal treatment for French. It also legislated immigrant children into French schools, and imposed language competency exams to test five-year-olds' knowledge of English. English-speaking voters, until that point overwhelmingly Liberal, were enraged.

Concerns for the future of French coincided with a drastic change in Quebec social behaviour. The decline in the standing of the Catholic church has already been noted. It was nowhere more noticeable or remarkable than in the question of the church's teachings on sex and reproduction. The invention of the birth control pill depressed reproduction rates throughout the western world, and Canada, where the pill began to be used in 1960, was no exception. The Catholic Church opposed the use of the pill as it did all other methods of contraception (except abstinence). Quebec, was the most officially Catholic section of Canada, but led the country in contraception, and the Quebec birthrate fell and continued falling, from 22 per 1,000 in the 1950s to 11.3 per 1,000 in 1997. Ontario, by comparison, moved from 17.1 per 1,000 in the 1950s to 12.3 per 1,000 in 1997.

Under the circumstances, immigration became crucial to Quebec's future, as did the assimilation of immigrants to the French rather than English community in Quebec. Yet paradoxically enforced use of French was a deterrent to immigration, because most immigrants to Canada believed they were coming to an English-speaking continent, where the use of English was not merely socially desirable but economically advantageous. There were very few sources of French-speaking immigrants (although in the 1970s immigration from Haiti did begin to pick up). The Ottawa government disapproved of Bourassa's language edicts: in 1976 Trudeau let it be generally known that he despised the Quebec premier as hopelessly weak and floundering.

Demography had become a cause for anxiety, and anxiety is a politically volatile commodity. Bourassa, himself anxious, was the worst person to prescribe a remedy, or to navigate past a political ambush.

THE QUEBEC REFERENDUM OF 1980

Beset by labour troubles, confused by the language question, and antagonized by its Liberal cousins in Ottawa, the Quebec Liberal government called a general election for November 1976. It lost badly. English-language voters deserted it because of the restrictions placed on the use of English, while many French-language voters voted against it because they believed Bourassa had not gone far enough.

René Lévesque led the separatist Parti Québécois into government. The PQ election platform was carefully nuanced to downplay separatism and appeal to those who merely thought Bourassa's Liberals a bad government. Lévesque proposed 'sovereignty-association,' as he had done since 1967, but only after a referendum authorizing him to negotiate the idea with Ottawa, and after a second referendum which would review the results of the negotiation. Only then, after two votes, could Quebec become independent.

It was hardly a ringing endorsement for separation, but it brought separation into the realm of the possible for the first time. The

Canadian dollar fell on international markets, Trudeau formed an emergency taskforce to coordinate the federal response and English Quebeckers assessed their prospects. In the latter case, these were limited, for one of the first actions of the PQ government was to bring in language legislation of a new and stringent kind. All companies over a certain size must set up 'francization' committees, all municipalities with 50 per cent plus one French population must conduct their official business in French only, all public signs (with a few exceptions, such as for churches) must also be in French only. To enforce the law, the government established an *Office de la langue française*, whose inspectors were promptly dubbed 'the language police' or 'the tongue troopers.' Soon a succession of small shopkeepers were served with summonses, and language cases began to wend their way toward the Canadian Supreme Court.

The most perceptible, and perhaps the most serious, effect of the political furore in Quebec and the resultant language legislation was the outflow of the province's English-language population. That population had always been mobile, but in the 1970s the mobility increased, and in one direction only – out. Many English-speaking Quebeckers are estimated to have left between 1976 and 1986. At the same time, the rate of immigration into Quebec fell, and those who came were officially encouraged to assimilate to the French-speaking majority. The result was a demographic catastrophe for Quebec's English speakers, whose children, finding that they could not get jobs and facing what they often (quite accurately) took to be hostility, left. Again, the statistics tell the story. In 1971, before the language legislation, English-speaking Quebeckers (by mother tongue) numbered 789,000; in 1981, there were 706,000; in 1996, there were 586,000.

Lévesque's principal objective was to secure a mandate to negotiate separation. Prime Minister Trudeau's main thought was to prevent such a development. Lévesque had a majority in the Quebec legislature, while Trudeau not only had a majority in Ottawa since a federal election in 1974, but the overwhelming majority of federal seats in Quebec. Lévesque's majority was more recent, and he could outwait Trudeau, who as it happened lost his majority and an election in May 1979. His place as prime minister was taken by the federal Conservative leader, Joe Clark, a young man, age 40, from Alberta. Clark led, moreover, a minority government, with almost no seats in Quebec. The circumstances seemed favourable, and Lévesque set his referendum machinery in motion. He was aiming for a spring vote, in May 1980.

Through a series of accidents, most of them his own fault, Clark lost a confidence vote in the House of Commons in December 1979. He then lost a general election to a rejuvenated Trudeau, in February 1980. 'Welcome to the 1980s,' Trudeau grinned on election night.

Trudeau, assisted by his lieutenant, Jean Chrétien, and the provincial Liberal leader, Claude Ryan, directed the referendum campaign of the spring of 1980 on the federal side. Lévesque naturally led the separatist troops, according to a strategy devised by his constitutional minister, Claude Morin. Admired but not loved, Trudeau prevailed in argument and prestige over Lévesque, loved but not respected. Trudeau promised a Canada that would work better and constitutional reforms to an electorate that was already inclined in his direction. On referendum night, May 20 1980, Trudeau won – by 60 per cent to 40 per cent, with a majority of French speakers voting for the federal option.

The Reform of the Constitution

Trudeau had always taken a certain interest in the Canadian constitution, but usually to explain that it was fine as it was. Realistically, however, he had to take into account the fact that many Canadians had come to believe that the solution to their problems with Quebec, and other problems too, lay with tinkering with the 1867 document. Provincial premiers outside Quebec found Quebec's discontent useful as a means to pry new powers out of the federal government. Twice, in 1971 and in 1978, they found the federal government inclined to agree, only to have agreement escape them because Quebec was inclined to go one or two or many steps beyond.

Trudeau, fresh from a general election victory in February 1980 and a referendum triumph in May, did not feel that he had to compromise. Lévesque did not speak for Quebec; he, Trudeau, did. What Trudeau wanted to was to situate the power to amend the Canadian constitution in Canada, and not in Great Britain, where it still resided. Bringing the constitution home was called 'patriation,' a new word. A former civil rights lawyer, he also hoped to secure a Canadian bill of rights on the American model, guaranteeing the freedoms of the citizen. To get it, he relied on a legal convention whereby the British government accepted the advice of its Canadian counterpart, one sovereign government to another, and refused to look behind the Canadian request to see whether the provinces agreed or not.

The Canadian provinces emphatically did not agree. Eight of them, including Quebec, opposed Trudeau's constitutional package when it was unveiled. They fought it in the courts, and when they lost there, took their case to Great Britain. The British prime minister, Margaret Thatcher, did not like Trudeau ('a wet') and she did not like bills of rights, which might create an unfortunate precedent in Great Britain. When Trudeau's constitutional amendments, complete with a Charter of Rights and Freedoms, threatened to arrive, she did everything within the bounds of diplomatic propriety (and a few things outside) to persuade him not to place this burden on her.

At the last moment Trudeau secured the agreement of all the provinces but one to a revised constitutional document, but one that still included the Charter of Rights and Freedoms. It was duly mailed to

Pierre Trudeau and Queen Elizabeth II at the signing of the revised Canadian constitution in 1982

London, and eventually passed. It returned to Canada to be signed into law by Elizabeth II in a ceremony in Ottawa on 17 April 1982.

The one dissenting province, of course, was Quebec. In the eyes of the Quebec government and of some observers outside Quebec, Trudeau had pulled off a constitutional coup, legal but illegitimate because it did not carry the consent of Quebec's government. To this objection, Trudeau's response was that he represented Quebec on this issue, and that he, not Lévesque, had won the 1980 referendum.

Public opinion polls showed support for separatism in Quebec receding, and a disposition to accept the constitution, not enthusiastically, but as a consequence of Lévesque's referendum defeat in 1980. Even Lévesque put separatism on a back burner; until his retirement from politics in 1985 he had essentially no constitutional platform.

That other political flashpoint, language, also receded. Lévesque's language legislation had the positive result of reassuring those French Quebeckers panicked by the possibility that their language would disappear. The price, it was true, was paid by the English-language community, declining and embittered; and it was probably reflected in lower levels of immigration and investment. For a brief period the Quebec problem was on hold and Canadians, including Quebeckers, turned to deal with other issues.

CHAPTER EIGHT

Ending the Century

The end of the twentieth century was, for Canadians, startlingly reminiscent of its beginning. English and French Canadians still worked together, grumbling, inside a common constitutional framework. The Canadian political system held the constitution together, allowing a parliamentary monarchy to function on the unfriendly soil of North America. Prosperity, nearly continuous, watered the growth of a social welfare system that as it grew and flourished appeared to define an important difference between Canada and the United States. Yet as that difference increased in importance, so did a steady economic rapprochement between Canada and the United States that according to some observers left Canada more, not less, American at the century's end.

The social welfare system, in its late century form, was the creation of the Liberal government of Lester B. Pearson. But Pearson was soon gone, retired in 1968, after recruiting if not creating a most unlikely successor. Working with Pearson's legacy, Pierre Trudeau (prime minister 1968–79 and 1980–84) fashioned his own and, his followers believed, reshaped the country in a definitive way in the process. From the 1960s to the 1990s the dominant political figure in Canada was Pierre Elliott Trudeau. Lavishly admired or bitterly loathed, in office or out, Trudeau shaped Canada as no politician had since Mackenzie King, or the distant Laurier or Macdonald.

Pearson's Legacy

The Liberal Pearson government (1963–68) came into office determined to complete the Canadian welfare state. In the 1963 election,

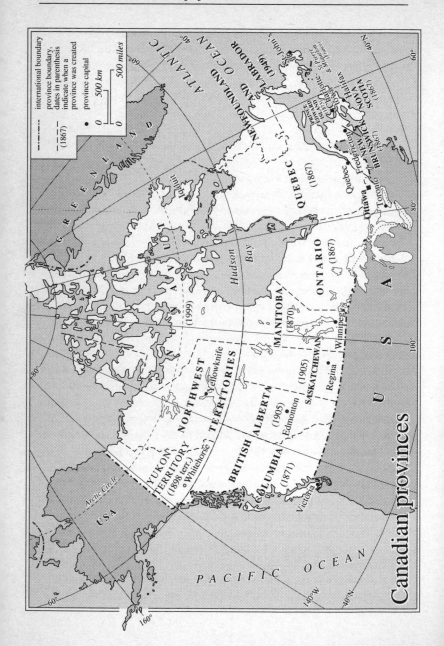

Canadian provinces

Pearson proposed to reform the pension system for the elderly, create a universal, state-paid health care system and to help university students through a generous system of loans guaranteed by the government. Over the next five years he largely succeeded, despite the fact that under the Canadian constitution questions of health and welfare lie in provincial rather than federal jurisdiction.

Navigating pensions past the provinces required some skill, but eventually a Canada Pension Plan was established (along with a parallel Quebec Pension Plan that underlined that province's jealous regard for its own jurisdiction). Canadians paid into a common fund, from which they would eventually draw old age pensions; in the meantime, however, the provinces had access to the money to finance their own schemes.

Next, a federally funded (but provincially administered) health scheme was founded, that would pay doctors' bills and hospital costs for all Canadians. Patients remained free to select their own doctors, and doctors remained free to prescribe whatever treatment they wished, secure in the knowledge that with the government paying the bills there would be no more defaulting debtors on their rolls. Doctors' incomes rose under the health care scheme, which Canadians called Medicare (not to be confused with the American government's Medicare, which paid for medical services only for the elderly). The key to securing provincial cooperation was abundant federal finance – an offer so good that the provinces could not resist.

The government spent money on universities and professors too, and for buildings and research, in addition to the student loan scheme. Again, federal largesse was the key. Unemployment insurance was expanded, and federal money flowed not merely to disadvantaged people, but to disadvantaged regions. Committed to ironing out inequalities among people, the government proposed to equalize the opportunities of whole regions, such as backwoods Quebec or the Atlantic Provinces. Instead of bringing people to jobs, Ottawa proposed to bring jobs to people, using incentives of all kinds, including outright subsidies.

The money came from abundant prosperity and from an economy that was growing at between 4 and 5 per cent a year. As long as the bonanza continued, Canada could easily afford what had been an unrealizable dream in the past, a cradle to grave welfare state, accessible to all.

In social policy, the Trudeau government (1968–79 and 1980–84) was the true inheritor of Pearson's initiatives. Pierre Trudeau, to the annoyance of some of his ministers, believed that government had an obligation to contribute to social justice, following the ideas of the Canadian expatriate economist, John Kenneth Galbraith. In regional economic development, unemployment insurance, Medicare and education subsidies, the Liberals proved remarkably consistent. The only drawback was that the economy that supported the system was less consistent.

TRADE AND INVESTMENT

As a diplomat, Pearson necessarily saw Canada in an international context. The trouble was that the international system was shifting away from the predictable realities of his youth, when the British Empire dominated the globe and reliably bought half of Canada's exports while funnelling in investment funds to expand the Canadian economy. After 1945 Britain's share of Canadian trade had dwindled, while British investment shrank as Britain's economic troubles multiplied. Fortunately there was an alternative. Canada enjoyed the inestimable advantage of sitting right next to the United States, the economic powerhouse of the late twentieth century. American money poured across the border, buying up Canadian firms and establishing new ones. The inflow of American investment funds also paid for American imports, on which Canadian industry as well as Canadian consumers depended. The result was an ever greater resemblance and even convergence between Canadian and American business, and between the Canadian and American economies. Intellectuals fretted, but Canadian workers knew very well that their industries and their jobs depended on a close and reliable relationship with the United States.

The Liberal Party and the Pearson government worried about what came to be called 'American economic domination.' In particular, Pearson's minister of finance, Walter Gordon, a Toronto politician, tried to devise ways that would lessen American influence, by using taxes and regulations to limit the sale of Canadian assets to Americans. Gordon's efforts were unpopular with the business community, which ultimately undermined his tenure as finance minister. Ironically, before he left office at the end of 1965 he presided over a major advance in Canadian-American economic integration.

Canada had had an automobile industry since the first decade of the twentieth century. Large automobile factories dominated the landscape of several southern Ontario cities, notably Windsor, Oshawa and Oakville. These factories belonged to the 'Big Three' American auto makers, Ford, General Motors and Chrysler, and they made short Canadian production runs for popular American car models. The industry was large, but it was also inefficient and costly, and Canadian consumers paid the penalty in higher prices for cars and less choice in what they bought. In terms of the balance of payments, automobiles were a regular and substantial drain; and in any case Canada had never had a favourable balance of payments with the United States.

Negotiations between Canadian and American trade diplomats in 1964 produced a radical suggestion: why not abolish all tariffs in the automotive sector, allowing free trade in automobiles and automobile parts. The Canadians, initially reluctant, agreed when the Americans allowed them to safeguard a minimum of automobile production in Canada. The car companies, all American-owned, and the labour unions, the same on both sides of the border, cooperated. In 1965 Pearson and America's President Lyndon Johnson signed a so-called Autopact that opened the border. Little noticed at the time, except in the car-producing communities, the Autopact revolutionized car production in Canada, and altered the balance of economic relations with the United States.

At first, while car manufacturing grew, the imbalance of payments continued as it always had: Canadians bought more from the United States than Americans bought in Canada. Soon, however, things changed. In 1970 Canada showed a slight surplus in automobile trade and then, a few years later, it happened again. The balance shifted, as Canadian factories produced some popular car models for the whole North American market.

Lester B. Pearson and Lyndon B. Johnson: their 'Autopact' revolutionalized car
production in Canada

That was significant enough, but even more important were the
sheer size and rate of growth of the automotive sector. In 1965 the
United States enjoyed a surplus of $703 million in the auto trade,
reflecting low Canadian auto exports to the United States. By 1968 this
had turned into a $22 million Canadian surplus and by 1972, the
balance in Canada's favour was $527 million. Employment – mostly in
Ontario – in automobile manufacturing rose from 70,000 in 1965 to
125,000 in 1978. Sales to the United States propelled production, and
as exports to that country rose, the shape of Ontario's economy shifted.
Until 1965 Ontario's largest customer was Quebec – and vice-versa. As
sales to the United States increased, the relative importance of exports
to the rest of Canada declined.

Much of Canada's official trade effort was directed elsewhere than
the United States. Canada had been a member of the General
Agreement on Tariffs and Trade since its founding in 1947, and
strongly supported the GATT's commitment to lowering trade barriers (in those days mainly tariffs) around the world. But the GATT
worked slowly; until the 1960s Canadian trade representatives para-

doxically succeeded in limiting and delaying reductions to the Canadian tariff.

For political reasons – the Cold War, and the fear that an unstable Europe was the breeding ground of war – Canada supported the establishment of a European trading bloc. First there was the European Common Market, in 1957, which evolved into the European Economic Community (EEC) and, eventually, in 1991, the European Union. Great Britain, Canada's principal transatlantic trading partner, struggled against economic logic and American pressure, but eventually, in 1973, joined the EEC. Canada then lost what remained of its preferred position in the British market, and failed to gain any compensating advantage in Europe. Dominated by French agricultural protectionism and fuelled by lavish subsidies, the European Community in effect told Canada to look elsewhere. A futile attempt in the 1970s to create some kind of special link between Canada and Europe changed the atmospherics but had no practical issue. Neither did sporadic aid and trade missions to the underdeveloped countries of the world.

Increasingly bound to the United States by trade, Canada by the 1980s came to view the situation, if not as politically desirable, then as politically and economically inevitable.

UNBALANCED FEDERALISM

Pierre Trudeau did not originally seek office to reform the Canadian constitution. The constitution worked as well as could be expected, he argued, and there was no reason to think that it could be substantially improved. As minister of justice under Pearson he began an exploration, with the provinces, to see whether the constitution could be amended. As prime minister, in 1971, he almost succeeded in cobbling together a package of amendments that did not unduly weaken federal power while establishing a procedure for amending the constitution, without the embarrassing necessity of seeking the consent of the British parliament. The nine mainly English-speaking provinces cooperated in the hope that an agreed constitutional change would appease Quebec. At the last moment Bourassa of Quebec pulled back, and Trudeau abandoned the exercise.

As we have seen (above, page 134) Trudeau returned to the charge in 1980. By 1980, however, Ottawa had problems not merely with Quebec, but with oil-rich Alberta. The spectacular rise in world oil prices in the 1970s had greatly benefited Alberta while unbalancing Ontario, Quebec, Manitoba and the Atlantic provinces. Trudeau's attempts to tap into Alberta's oil wealth were resented as a blatant attempt to poach on western Canadian territory. 'Let the Eastern Bastards Freeze in the Dark,' Alberta bumper stickers explained.

For a time, comparisons were drawn between Quebec's (or the Quebec government's) desire to separate from Canada and Alberta's desire to insulate its oil riches from eastern Canadians. In the end, however, the English-speaking provinces – all of them – came together and struck a deal with Trudeau for the amendment of the constitution, leaving Quebec outside. Reaction to the constitutional deal of 1982 in Canada excluding Quebec (and even to some extent within Quebec) showed that Trudeau had caught the national mood with his Charter of Rights and Freedoms. The Charter joined Medicare as an item that Canadians identified with, and Trudeau's personal stature, as the man who had achieved the revised constitution, increased, even as his political fortunes plummetted. In the euphoria, few people noticed a small compromise that Trudeau had made to get his charter. Parliament and provincial legislatures were granted the power to overrule the Charter and its provisions, provided they said that that was what they were doing, and for a limited but renewable five-year term. This was called the 'notwithstanding' clause. If governments were to abrogate certain rights enforceable under the Charter, in other words, they would have to say so and take the resulting political heat. It seemed a safe bet that governments would seldom if ever use the power.

IMMIGRATION, MULTICULTURALISM AND CIVIL SOCIETY

Viewed from outside, Canada was a most attractive country in the 1970s and 1980s. Prosperous, well ordered, with large, clean cities and a liberally inclined government, Canada was a favoured destination for migrants. After World War II, and down through the 1960s, most arrivals in Canada came from Europe. As western and northern Europe recovered economically after the war, southern Europeans came to predominate. Italians became a visible presence in Montreal and Toronto especially, followed by Portuguese and Greeks. In the 1970s, the balance shifted further south and west, to the Caribbean and across the Pacific to Asia. The Asian component of the Canadian population grew rapidly, with immigration from India and China. Refugees came too, lured by a country that prided itself on a liberal refugee policy: Indians expelled from East Africa in the 1970s, Somalis fleeing war and civil war and Central Americans fleeing oppression and civil war in the 1980s.

The Liberal Party, in power from 1963 to 1984, drew much of its strength from immigrant communities. Some Liberals even saw their party as a coalition of minorities, real or perceived, and worked to implant the minorities' image on Canada. Canada, they argued, was not a melting pot like the United States, and never had been. Canada was a country of many cultures, none predominant or official. The Trudeau government conceived and passed into law a Multiculturalism Act, designed to recognize and encourage various ethnic communities to be themselves, albeit in the context of an English- and French-speaking state.

Critics condemned multiculturalism as undermining a sense of common citizenship, or, at best, as a futile exercise that attempted to turn back the tide of cultural homogenization. Ethnic groups, they pointed out, had always lived apart in their first generation on Canadian soil but, in the second generation and even more in the third, they would blend and adapt, dropping first the language of their immigrant parents and eventually all but a sentimental regard for a distant and unfamiliar homeland. Some even cast doubt on the notion that Canada was different from the United States in this regard – all immigrant countries, they argued, were melting pots.

Predictably the group most offended by multiculturalism was Quebec separatists, who feared for the future of their minority. Surely multiculturalism was a plot to make French Canadians one large ethnic group among many. Declining birthrates fed these fears: French Canadians as a group were dropping steadily from 28 per cent of the population in 1961 to 24 per cent in 1996. (The measure is by mother tongue.) Many French Canadians, and not only separatists, feared that the French-speaking communities outside Quebec would eventually melt and disappear too. If that happened, would not Quebec itself eventually follow the path of formerly French-speaking Louisiana, where French was on the verge of extinction by the 1990s?

Federalists pointed out that the United States was not a bilingual country and that the Canadian border had helped insulate French Canadians in a country where English was not the predominant language of 95 per cent, as in the United States, but of a mere 70 per cent, and those 70 per cent were accustomed to view the use of French as an integral part of their history and their present. The best way to insure the future, Trudeau and other federalists claimed, was not to upset the status quo, which acted to protect French, and thus a French-speaking Quebec.

Brian Mulroney

Between 1963 and 1984 the main vehicle for opposition to Pearson and Trudeau, and the Liberals, was the Progressive Conservative Party, the party of Sir John A. Macdonald. The Conservatives or Tories, as they were known after the British model, were a mainstream, omnibus party that aimed, like the Liberals, to include as many interests and therefore as many voters as possible. Against Trudeau they did not quite succeed, though they did manage to form a brief minority government under Joe Clark in 1979–80.

Clark fell in an internal Conservative coup in 1983. His successor was a Montreal labour lawyer and corporate executive, Brian Mulroney. Mulroney was an Irish Quebecker, fluent in both official languages, a born conciliator and deal maker, loyal to his friends, abundantly charming in private if slightly oleaginous in public. Mulroney, unlike Trudeau, was unburdened by a set of constitutional principles: he simply wanted to make Canada work, and he believed that his 'sunny ways,' like Laurier's 80 years before, were what Canada needed after Trudeau's abrasive and confrontational style.

In the event, Mulroney did not face Trudeau in an election, but a new Liberal prime minister, John Turner. Trudeau resigned as Liberal

Brian Mulroney, a landslide victory made him prime minister of a Conservative
government in 1984

Party leader in February 1984, and Turner succeeded him in June. The
Liberals, deceived by a temporary blip in their favour in public opinion
polls, promptly called an election for September and suffered the worst
electoral defeat in their history up to that time. Mulroney won over
half the popular vote, an immense parliamentary majority, and support
in every region of Canada, including and especially in Quebec. In
Quebec, the Conservatives displaced the Liberals as the party of choice,
ending almost 100 years of identification between French Canadians
and the Liberal Party.

The Conservatives under Mulroney were a breath of fresh air after
20 years of the Liberals, and many of the new ministers were both
imaginative and competent. Yet chance and circumstance forced the
Conservatives into policies that broadly speaking were not much different from those the Liberals had laid down. Trudeau's policies had left
a substantial burden of government debt that had to be paid or at least
serviced. Economies in other directions were politically unpalatable,
especially because Mulroney had described social programmes as a
'sacred trust.' The Canadian welfare state was not terminated or
privatized, nor did the government rush to privatize public assets, after

the model of the contemporary British prime minister, Margaret Thatcher. (Thatcher, however, was probably the first British political figure since Winston Churchill to make a serious impact on Canadian political thought and practice.)

FREE TRADE

Not every member of the Mulroney government was a model of high mindedness or good conduct, and a number of scandals marred Mulroney's term of office. Needing a public initiative to restore his government's fading image, Mulroney reached into the civil service for an idea that had been around as long as Canada.

In the last stages of the Trudeau government the Liberals had toyed with the idea of 'sectoral' free trade with the United States. This would have progressively extended the free trade of the Autopact to other 'sectors' of the economy. It was politically difficult to sell – especially to the Americans – and economically hard to define, and as a serious proposal it quickly died. Nevertheless the notion of sectoral free trade set minds working. There had been a serious recession in 1981–82, which undermined Canadians' confidence in the functioning of their economy, particularly in the business community. International trade negotiations stalled during the 1980s. Other trade blocs were forming, excluding Canada. There were fears that the United States might choose to solve its own economic problems by capriciously restricting trade with Canada.

The American government was receptive. Free trade with Canada would stimulate the lowering of tariffs worldwide, or so it was thought. The administration of Ronald Reagan was publicly committed to some kind of initiative that would bind Mexico and Canada closer to their neighbour, the United States. The president liked Mulroney, who lost no time in assuring the Americans that Canada was their best friend. The time seemed right, and in 1985 Mulroney and Reagan announced that negotiations would begin on a free trade pact between Canada and the United States.

The negotiations were long and difficult. The Americans, it quickly developed, did not want free trade nearly as much as Canada did. Mulroney wanted a system that would stabilize Canadian-American trade and insulate it against sudden American restrictions. Eventually, at the last minute in October 1987, politicians on both sides had to intervene to secure a deal. It abolished tariffs between Canada and the United States over a ten-year period and provided for a system of bilateral, quasi-judicial panels that would rule on whether American trade laws that might restrict imports from Canada were being applied fairly.

Despite their massive majority in the House of Commons, Mulroney's Conservatives were in a minority in the appointed Senate. The Liberal leader, John Turner, made it plain that the Liberals would block the ratification of the free trade treaty in the Senate. He wanted an election on the issue, and finally Mulroney had to oblige.

The election of November 1988 was one of the most dramatic in Canadian history. There was substantial opposition from Canadian nationalists, who feared that political absorption would follow economic integration. The business community, which in 1891 and 1911 had been hostile to free trade with the United States, now grasped at the idea as their best hope for economic salvation. The nationalists had votes, but the vote was divided between the Liberals and the New Democratic Party, Canada's version of social democracy. A televised debate among the leaders of Canada's political parties reduced Mulroney to spluttering incoherence and allowed Turner to rally the anti-free trade, nationalist forces in Canada around his own Liberal Party. The Canadian dollar shivered on international markets and a sudden infusion of cash from the business community was translated into a Conservative media blitz that predicted economic ruin if the Liberals prevailed. As important, the NDP vote, though reduced during the election, was still sizeable. The result was a substantially reduced Conservative majority, but a majority nonetheless. Reagan and Mulroney formally signed free trade into law on 1 January 1989.

A New Quebec Crisis

Separatist feeling in Quebec reached a low ebb following the unsuccessful referendum on separation in 1980. In 1982 Trudeau was able to ram his amendment of the Canadian constitution into law, repatriating the constitution and establishing the Charter of Rights and Freedoms without any compensating concessions to the provinces and, especially, any increase in Quebec's jurisdiction. The separatist provincial government of René Lévesque tried to rally opinion against Trudeau, but it was a hopeless task. In the 1984 referendum, Quebec nationalists, including most separatists, put their hope and their votes into the Conservative Party of Brian Mulroney, who was at least not their hated adversary, Trudeau.

Mulroney, as a prominent Quebecker, had opposed separatism in the 1980 referendum. As prime minister of Canada, his first task was to prevent the recurrence of the separatist agitation of the 1960s and 1970s. At the same time, he saw an opportunity to reintegrate former separatists and Quebec nationalists generally into the Canadian political system, using his party as a vehicle for what he saw as a moderate alternative. When the Quebec Liberal Party, committed to federalism, returned to power in 1985 under Robert Bourassa, he saw an opportunity, which he promptly seized.

Appeasing Quebec was not a bad idea in principle. Bourassa's price was high, but not unreasonably so: it would have transferred appointments to the Senate and the Canadian Supreme Court, previously strictly federal, partly to the provinces, and would have recognized Quebec as a 'distinct society.' The western provinces were attracted by the idea of Senate reform, and hoped in future discussions to secure an elected upper chamber with equal representation from each province, along the model of the United States Senate. But at the time it was 'Quebec's turn,' and western aspirations were put on hold, to await a future, but obligatory, constitutional conference. (This was one of the unusual features of the Mulroney constitutional package, which would have put Canada into a continuous state of constitutional review.) The federal and provincial governments unanimously agreed to Mulroney's constitutional reforms at a meeting at a federal guest house outside Ottawa, at Meech Lake, in April 1987, and at a final, confirmatory, session in Ottawa in June. The deal, announced with much fanfare, had to be ratified by all the provinces and by the federal parliament by June 1990. At the time, it seemed like an easy target.

Instead, the Meech Lake Agreement fell apart. There were a number of reasons. The most important was the interpretation of the clause that made Quebec legally a 'distinct society.' It changed nothing, Mulroney and his allies told the public; all it did was confirm Quebec's existing distinctiveness – its French language, its different system of laws, and so forth. That was not, however, what Bourassa told his followers in Quebec. 'Distinct society' would enshrine Quebec's language laws, and, better still, could be used to pry more powers and jurisdiction from a federal government that would now be obliged to treat Quebec differently. From this point of view, Meech Lake was half way to separatism, and who knew what future negotiations, promised in the proposed constitution, would bring?

Canadians received a foretaste of what Bourassa meant by 'distinct' in October 1987. The Canadian Supreme Court ruled that certain portions of Quebec's language law conflicted with the Charter of Rights and Freedoms. Quebec was accordingly instructed to alter its practice and in this case to allow English-language signs, accompanied by a larger French version, to appear in public.

Bourassa did not hesitate. Believing that any abatement in Quebec's language legislation would upset the 'social peace' of the province, he used the 'notwithstanding clause' of the 1982 constitution to reverse the court's decision. English Canadians generally condemned Bourassa's action; French Canadians generally supported it. Once again, along the fault line of language, Canadians differed. Meech Lake immediately became a much more difficult case to sell, outside of Quebec.

Opponents of the Meech Lake deal had a leader. In a savage newspaper article, Pierre Trudeau damned Mulroney's compromises, which he argued would neither satisfy Quebec nationalists nor benefit the country. Mulroney and the premiers were weaklings and fools, Trudeau proclaimed, and must be repudiated. When, in 1989, one of Trudeau's admirers was elected premier of Newfoundland, displacing the previous government, Meech's opponents acquired the means to dispose of the obnoxious proposal. Newfoundland's legislature rescinded its approval of the constitutional amendments; Manitoba's had never passed them. Mulroney frantically tried to stick Meech Lake together again in a series of conferences in the spring of 1990, but he had waited too long and had too little with which to bargain. In June 1990 Meech Lake was dead.

The reaction in Quebec, where Bourassa's dubious role in Meech Lake's defeat was ignored and unacknowledged, was an outburst of rage. Even moderate French Canadians saw the rejection as a slap in the face of Quebec. Separatism, previously almost dead, soared; federalism plumbed the depths. Had a referendum been held in 1990 or 1991, federalism's defeat would have been assured.

Bourassa, previously ambiguous on the nationalist side, now turned his talent to rescue federalism in his province. Sinuously he stimulated compromise proposals, suggested a referendum if Quebec's needs were not met and postponed and delayed. Separatists and those outraged by the failure of Meech Lake were allowed to blow off steam in public hearings. Meanwhile the federal government commissioned hearings of its own and eventually, with the cooperation of the provinces and native representatives, produced yet another constitutional design, called the Charlottetown proposal after the city where the deal was finally put together in the summer of 1992.

It would be fair to say that nobody was quite certain what the Charlottetown proposal meant, or what it would have done. No-one would ever find out, because it was rejected in a national referendum in October 1992, by 54 per cent to 46 per cent. Quebec joined western Canada in turning thumbs down. Mulroney's attempt to review and revise the Canadian constitution had failed.

The Meech Lake experience was a serious blow to the government's prestige in the short term, besides a threat to the existence of the country. The financial situation drove Mulroney into another policy, fiscally necessary, which also weighed down the government. A new federal sales tax, called the Goods and Services Tax (a version of the European Value Added Tax), replaced an older and burdensome tax on manufactures. The GST promised to alleviate pressure on the government's finances just at the point when a new economic recession in 1990–91 was driving revenues down. The trouble with the GST was that it was collected at the point of final sale, and was therefore highly visible; it was also cumbersome to administer, requiring its own staff and collection services.

The Liberals fought this tax tooth and nail, ostensibly for the public good but also because it is the function of an opposition to oppose. In this case, opposition was the right political move, and the Liberals, already benefiting from their opposition to free trade, steadily pulled away from the Conservatives in public opinion polls. The Liberals took advantage of the novelty of a new leader, veteran of Trudeau's cabinets, Jean Chrétien. Where Mulroney's characteristic style was over-statement if not ostentation, Chrétien had a reputation as a plain man of the people.

In the spring of 1993 Mulroney, testing the political winds and finding them unfavourable, chose to retire. After enduring an orgy of self-congratulation on the achievements of Mulroney and his government, a Conservative convention chose Kim Campbell, one of Mulroney's ministers, to succeed him. Campbell was Canada's first woman prime minister, and she had an engaging if sometimes unconsidered approach to her task. That task, it soon became apparent, was hopeless. Mulroney had managed to become the most unpopular politician in Canadian history, far surpassing R. B. Bennett in the 1930s.

With Parliament at the end of its five-year term, Campbell had to call an election in October 1993. In the result, she was personally defeated in her home constituency in Vancouver, and her party lost all but two seats in the House of Commons. It was much more a judgement on the Conservatives than a ratification of the Liberals, who got a solid but not massive majority. The Liberals shared the new Parliament with three other parties. There were New Democrats, who lost seats but retained a toehold, the Reform Party, a conservative-populist aggregation that drew most of its strength from British Columbia, Alberta and Saskatchewan, and the Bloc Québécois, a separatist party from Quebec under the leadership of another Mulroney ex-minister, a disillusioned nationalist named Lucien Bouchard.

The Chrétien Government

The Chrétien government, like its predecessor, was largely the prisoner of circumstances. Except on the subject of Canadian unity the prime minister had no very strong views, yet it was in the area of national unity that Chrétien was weakest. A populist politician from a small city in the heart of Quebec, Chrétien did not appeal to urban intellectuals who formed the backbone of the province's media. A strong federalist, he had not supported Meech Lake and thereby earned the indifference if not the outright hostility of Bourassa and his provincial Liberals. In the 1993 election the Liberals won fewer seats in Quebec than they had in 1984 or 1988 – only 19, mostly in areas with a substantial English or immigrant population. On the other hand, the Liberals won all but one of Ontario's seats, and substantial representation elsewhere in the country, enabling them to claim that they were the only remaining national party.

Chrétien drew the conclusion from Canada's recent experience that a successful amendment to the constitution was unlikely, and that the chances of any amendment at all were slim. He did not therefore waste much time on the subject, trusting that efficient government and the return of prosperity would lighten the national mood.

The difficulty was that the federal deficit and the national debt had ballooned to alarming proportions, despite Mulroney's aggressive tax policy. There did not appear to be much room to raise taxes further, and further borrowing was imprudent. Chrétien, acting through his finance minister Paul Martin, made the difficult choice to restrain federal spending, which had to be done at the cost of popular programmes like Medicare. Because federal spending in areas of social and educational policy flowed through the provinces to the consumer, the provincial governments paid a price in political popularity. (They had always taken the lion's share of the credit for spending when spending was in fashion, so there was a rough justice in accepting some blame when the fiscal wheel turned.)

Recovery from the 1991 recession was slow, and the results were mixed. Unemployment remained high, moving from 10 per cent in 1991 to 11 per cent in 1993 to 7 per cent in 1999. Canada's record in this respect was better than most of Europe's; unemployment in France sat stubbornly at an average 9 per cent through the 1990s, and in Germany at 9 per cent as well. Canadians, however, compared themselves not with Europeans but with Americans, and in the United

States there were the lowest unemployment rates in 30 years. Americans' personal income and standards of living were rising, and taxes were low and getting lower.

For Chrétien and his ministers it was a race against time: to get the deficit under control, lower the national debt and, by lowering or eliminating federal borrowing, also lower interest rates. Progress in these areas would be measured against increasing taxpayer weariness, a reaction to more than a decade of steady tax increases with no apparent progress in reducing either deficit or debt.

There were worries over productivity, which was lower than in the United States, and fear of a brain drain to the south, as more and better jobs opened up south of the border. The Free Trade Agreement allowed skilled Canadians an opportunity for temporary employment in the United States, and many took advantage. Emigrants, permanent or temporary, were spurred by another consideration: Canadian living standards were falling in the 1990s as American living standards were rising. The resulting gap, the largest since the 1950s or 1960s, fed discontent.

The Chrétien government understood that in the circumstances Canadians were not inclined to take any major economic risks. The Mulroney Conservative government had signed the North American Free Trade Agreement (NAFTA), negotiated between the United States, Canada and Mexico. Chrétien had criticized the agreement but, on consideration, he withdrew his objection. The political advantage of a tripartite trade arrangement that brought in another partner was too great to ignored, even if there were serious concerns that Mexico, as a Third World country (though with a First World elite), was too dissimilar a society to be easily integrated. Chrétien may also have concluded that the real battle over free trade had been fought and lost in 1988; it was too late in 1993 to do anything but refine the details and adjust the balance.

In the circumstances it might be thought that the political position of the Chrétien government was weak. Perhaps, measured in terms of issues or resources, it was. But measured against an enfeebled, divided and generally incompetent opposition the Liberal government seemed to be in a strong position.

The Second Quebec Referendum

The major exception was Quebec. There, the provincial Liberals lost to the Parti Québécois, under Jacques Parizeau, an economist and a separatist warhorse, in 1994. Parizeau, unlike his predecessor René Lévesque in the 1970s, believed in sovereignty and was prepared to do without association with the rest of Canada. The Meech Lake fiasco had soured French-speaking Quebec opinion on Canada and created disarray among federalists. Parizeau's problem was the Quebec electorate, which was prepared to demonstrate irritation, even resentment, at the rest of Canada but which was not prepared to take the ultimate step of severing all ties. A second difficulty was that while Parizeau was admired for his intelligence, he was not liked for his pompous public style; even separatists infinitely preferred the fiery Lucien Bouchard, the separatists' leader in the federal parliament.

Parizeau would not compromise on a referendum. A vote there must be. He would, however, compromise on the question to be submitted to the electorate. If the Quebec electorate voted yes to his question, the separatist government would attempt to negotiate an economic association with Canada for a sovereign Quebec. It was a more attractive formulation, but the initial stages of the referendum campaign still went badly for the separatists. Parizeau had to swallow his pride and allow Bouchard to take his place as chief spokesman for the 'yes' side. Bouchard banished all doubts when he promised that independence from Canada would be 'a magic wand' that would banish the compromises and mediocrity of bilingual federalism in a glow of national unity.

Until Bouchard's intervention the federal campaign expected to win, and win by a majority similar to that in 1980, which was 60 to 40. Complacency and arrogance allowed the initiative to slip away, and when it did, panic took place. Non-French voters in Quebec understood that the future Quebec nation was being linguistically if not ethnically defined.

The result was very close. The federalist side eked out a bare majority, 50.6 per cent to 49.4 per cent. French-speaking voters had voted 60 to 40 for the prospect of independence, however it might be defined, while non-French had voted virtually 100 per cent against. The non-French total was swelled by the votes of the indigenous peoples of northern Quebec, whose leaders proclaimed that they would not be bound by the results of the referendum.

Parizeau promptly resigned, and was replaced by Lucien Bouchard as Parti Québécois chief and premier. Chrétien was in an awkward position, since it was plain that his influence over the referendum was at best slight, and at worst negative. It seemed, briefly, that the initiative was Bouchard's. Keeping the initiative, however, depended on keeping up the momentum of the separatist drive for a majority, and momentum was lacking. Bouchard found himself becalmed in government, and public opinion polls told him that virtually the last thing anyone wanted was another referendum.

Chrétien and Bouchard survived, with the likelihood of another confrontation in future, though when that day would be no-one could tell. Chrétien and his Liberal Party won a general election in June 1997, while Bouchard and his separatists won their own provincial election in November 1998. Bouchard promised another referendum if 'winning conditions' existed, meaning that he would call a vote only if he were certain of winning it.

ABORIGINAL ISSUES

For most of the twentieth century Canada's native peoples lingered on the margin of public affairs, outside the political mainstream, largely unrepresented in Canada's political system. At the beginning of the twentieth century, the aboriginal peoples seemed on the way to absorption in the general population or to disappearance: their numbers touched 105,000 in the 1911 census and grew slowly until the 1940s. In the 1950s and later, however, their numbers increased steadily, until by 1996 they numbered 800,000. Of these, some 234,000 spoke an aboriginal language (the most widely spoken being Cree). In some parts of Canada indigenous peoples were a large and growing presence, particularly in northern Ontario, Saskatchewan and Manitoba.

Under the Canadian constitution, native affairs belong to the federal government. Initially the government pursued a policy of isolation and

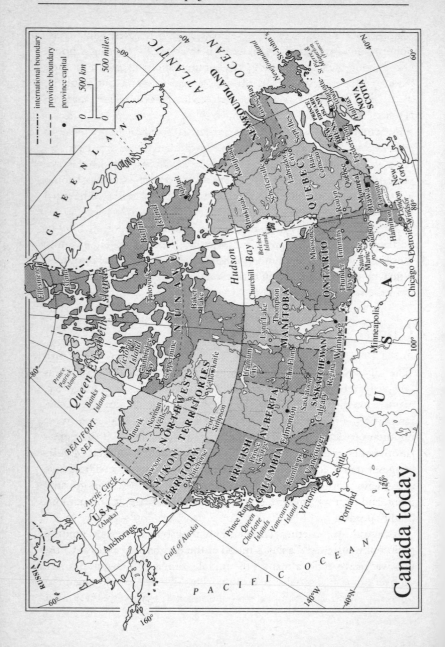

Canada today

assimilation – subsidies for those who stayed on reserves, while compulsorily educating native children off reserves in boarding schools, encouraging them to forget the ways of their ancestors, and even their parents. This policy was, on the whole, unsuccessful, but until the 1970s the objective remained the same: integrating natives into the larger society.

A change in the cultural climate in the 1970s and 1980s put a halt to assimilation as an official objective. Since then there has been no consensus, either among natives or among non-natives on what native policy should be. Should there be native self-government? If so, should it be municipal, provincial, or sovereign? Should there be differential treatment of natives, in law or in fact?

A tentative start may have been made with the creation in 1999 in northern Canada of a majority Inuit territory, called Nunavut, meaning 'our land.' Vast in extent but with distinctly limited financial resources, Nunavut holds out a promise that only substantial financial support from the south will fulfill.

Canada Today and Tomorrow

In the 1990s the United Nations' survey of world living conditions, 'The UN Human Development Index,' regularly reported Canada as one of the most fortunate places to live on earth. In terms of longevity, infant mortality, literacy and a variety of other measures, Canada ranked at the top, above the countries of western Europe and, most important to Canadians, above the United States. In 1999 the population was estimated at 30,491,246 with 26.17 per cent nineteen years of age or under, and about twelve per cent over sixty-five. These UN assessments were received with gratification by the Canadian government, and Prime Minister Chrétien predictably referred to them in his public speeches.

It was unclear whether Chrétien's political style or even his political philosophy matched Canada's mood at the end of the century. Chrétien was proverbially a man of the middle, prone to seek compromise on everything but Quebec separatism. His Liberal party occupied the middle of Canadian politics – a traditional Canadian party sought victory through compromise, by attracting as much of the middle ground as it could to itself. But could a party that sought to satisfy as many people as possible end up by satisfying any of them?

In the 1990s the political centre came under assault from the right wing. Right wing governments (nominally Progressive Conservative) emerged in Alberta and Ontario, especially, and their admirers hoped to duplicate their success on the national level. The western-based Reform party, which stood for less government and decentralization, converted itself into an amalgam with right-wing Conservatives, hoping to break through in populous Ontario, which by itself held 35 per cent of the seats in the House of Commons and was the key to electoral success. The resulting party was formed in the spring of 2000 and called itself the Canadian Alliance.

Prime Minister Chrétien promptly called an election in November 2000, and to the astonishment of many, he defeated the Canadian Alliance, and improved his Liberal party's standing in Quebec and the Atlantic provinces. It was his third straight majority, and a personal triumph; but it was more fundamentally a reaffirmation of the political fact that in a country as diverse and far-flung as Canada, only compromise and broad-based political formations can hope to prevail.

In Canada, a country where moderation is almost a public watchword, it was predictable that Canadians would be moderately content with their lot. Life was comfortable, taxes were gradually going down, the Chrétien government had abolished the federal deficit, at least temporarily, and there were few visible enemies, internal or external. Quebec separatism had been around so long that it had become a part of the political landscape, and when the Canadian Supreme Court ruled, as it did in 1998, that Quebec's separation, if it ever occurred, must conform to standards of fairness, and that fairness applied to both the federal side and the separatist camp, most people in Quebec and the rest of Canada nodded and got on with their business. The Quebec question thus lingered, an irritant but not an agony, and the question of Quebec's independence, if it were ever to occur, was postponed for the twenty-first century to handle.

Less predictable, and more problematic, was the future of Canada's native peoples; 400 years of contact with immigrants inevitably had their impact. Intermarriage, social and economic contact, deliberate government policies and the pressure of surrounding European communities all tended to homogenize indigenous societies; but physical separation, discrimination and poverty, not to mention the history and culture of native people, tended to keep them distinct.

Immigration too altered the face of Canada in the late twentieth century – visibly, because most of the immigrants in the 1980s and 1990s were nonwhite. Canadians vigorously disputed what this might mean. Immigrants tended to have their own answer, as they shed the languages of the countries they had left behind and searched for accommodation and equality in the society they had found and which they expected their children would help re-found.

Uncertainties about Canada's future path coincided with a flourishing cultural scene. Canadian writers in the late twentieth century reflected the country's metropolitan life, its immigrants and minorities, and the uneasy coexistence of its two principal languages. Robertson Davies' novels spanned Canada (mostly Ontario) from the 1940s to the 1980s, adding a psychological twist to the interpretation of English-Canadian life. Roch Carrier, on the French side, commanded attention with his portrayals of Canada's (and Quebec's) present and recent past. Roger Fournier, Yves Thériault, and Anne Hébert all maintained Quebec's literary culture and gave it a twentieth-century dimension. The Montreal writer Mordecai Richler wrote a series of novels centred on the Jewish community of Montreal; to the fury of Quebec separatists (whom he dubbed 'the woollies') he gave the world a scathing portrait of Quebec's language laws and their effect on the province's English-speakers.

Margaret Atwood, a Toronto writer, depicted her native city in a series of prizewinning novels (her awards included, in 2000, the Booker Prize). Alistair MacLeod movingly depicted the Scots of Cape Breton Island in his fiction, while Jane Urquhart did the same for the Irish immigrants to central Canada. Alice Munro, another Ontario writer, proved to be a master of the short story. From British Columbia, George Bowering, the poet P.K. Page, Spider Robinson and the playwright John Gray provided a vigorous competition to Ontario's cultural pretensions, while the Winnipeg writer Carol Shields won the

Pulitzer Prize for her fiction. W.P. Kinsella, an Alberta writer, wrote notable portraits of prairie life – and baseball. Rohinton Mistry and Michael Ondaatje, among others, chronicled Canadian life from an immigrant's perspective. In the English-speaking world, Toronto ranked behind only New York and London in number of theatres and theatrical productions.

No picture of Canada is complete without the United States. Present since Canada's creation, closely related by origin and experience and philosophy, the United States has been since 1945 Canada's major economic and political partner – a senior partner. Canadians, uncomfortably aware that to much of the rest of the world they are outwardly indistinguishable from Americans, have tended to magnify and sometimes exaggerate the differences that do exist between the two North American countries.

On the other hand, Canadians sometimes forget or omit, in their familiarity with the United States, its institutions and its cultures, the differences that 200 years of separation have made. Americans, detecting identical streetscapes, a common language and predictable reactions, sometimes react as if Canada was a northern extension of Iowa or Oregon. Canadians and Americans have much in common and have followed parallel paths, but, in matters large and small, they have not been quite the same. Nor, in the twenty-first century, is the difference likely to vanish.

Notes

Governors-General of Canada from 1867

Viscount Monck   *1861–1868*
Lord Lisgar   *1868–1872*
Earl of Dufferin   *1872–1878*
Marquess of Lorne   *1878–1883*
Marquess of Lansdowne   *1883–1888*
Lord Stanley   *1888–1893*
Earl of Aberdeen   *1893–1898*
Earl of Minto   *1898–1904*
Earl Grey   *1904–1911*
Prince Arthur, Duke of Connaught   *1911–1916*
Duke of Devonshire   *1916–1921*
Lord Byng   *1921–1926*
Viscount Willingdon   *1926–1931*
Earl of Bessborough   *1931–1935*
Lord Tweedsmuir   *1935–1940*
Earl of Athlone   *1940–1946*
Viscount Alexander   *1946–1952*
Vincent Massey   *1952–1959*
Georges-Philéas Vanier   *1959–1967*
Roland Michener   *1967–1974*
Jules Léger   *1974–1979*
Edward R. Schreyer   *1979–1984*
Jeanne Sauvé   *1984–1990*
Ramon John Hnatyshyn   *1990–1995*
Roméo LeBlanc   *1995–1999*
Adrienne Clarkson   *1999–Present*

26

Governors and Governors in Chief of Quebec, Lower Canada and Canada, 1760–1861

James Murray   *1760–1768*
Sir Guy Carleton   *1768–1778*
Sir Frederick Haldimand   *1778–1786*
Lord Dorchester   *1786–1796*
Robert Prescott   *1797–1807*
Sir James Craig   *1807–1811*
Sir George Prevost   *1811–1815*
Sir John Sherbrooke   *1816–1818*
Duke of Richmond   *1818–1819*
Earl of Dalhousie   *1820–1828*
Lord Aylmer   *1831–1835*
Earl Amherst   *1835*
Earl of Gosford   *1835–1837*
Earl of Durham   *1838*
Sir John Colborne   *1839*
Charles Thompson (Lord Sydenham)   *1839–1841*
Sir Charles Bagot   *1841–1843*
Sir Charles Metcalfe   *1843–1845*
Earl Cathcart   *1846–1847*
Earl of Elgin   *1847–1854*
Sir Edmund Head   *1854–1861*

French Governors 1627–1760

Samuel de Champlain   *1627–1635*
Charles de Montmagny   *1635–1648*
Louis d'Ailleboust de Coulonge
    1648–1651
Jean de Lauzon   *1651–1657*
Vicomte d'Argenson   *1658–1661*
Baron d'Avaugour   *1661–1663*
Augustin de Mésy   *1663–1665*
Daniel de Courcelle   *1665–1672*
Comte de Frontenac   *1672–1682*
Comte de Frontenac   *1689–1698*
Joseph-Antoine de La Barre   *1682–1685*

Marquis de Denonville   *1685–1689*
Hector de Callière   *1698–1703*
Philippe de Vaudreuil   *1703–1725*
Marquis de Beauharnois   *1726–1747*
Comte de La Galissonnière   *1747–1749*
Marquis de La Jonquière   *1749–1752*
Marquis de Duquesne   *1752–1755*
Pierre de Vaudreuil   *1755–1760*

Lieutenant Governors of Cape Breton Island 1784–1820

Cape Breton Island was given its independence from the Nova Scotia government between 1784 and 1820. While there were lieutenant governors for some of this period, it seems that for most of the time, there were 'presidents of council' who fulfilled the same role. This is according to Richard Brown in *A History of the Island of Cape Breton*, written in 1869. Except for the first and third names in the list, only the military rank and last name of the men are listed by Brown. These presidents of council were appointed by either the British crown itself or by representatives in the colonies. Listed here are both lieutenant governors and presidents of council:

Major Frederic Wallet Desbarres	Lieutenant Governor	*May 1784–Oct 1787*
Lieutenant Colonel Macormick	Lieutenant Governor	*Oct 1787–May 1795*
David Mathews	Attorney General and Senior Councillor (Interim Leader)	*May 1795–Jun 1798*
Brigadier General Ogilvie	President of Council	*Jun 1798–Jun 1799*
Brigadier General Murray	President of Council	*Jun 1799–Sep 1800*
Major General Despard	President of Council	*Sep 1800–Jul 1807*
Brigadier General Nepean	President of Council	*Jul 1807–Dec 1812*
Brigadier General Swayne	President of Council	*Jan 1813–Feb 1816*
Lieutenant Colonel Fitzherbert	President of Council	*Feb 1816–Nov 1816*
Major General Ainslie	Lieutenant Governor	*Nov 1816–Jun 1820*

Lieutenant Governors of New Brunswick 1784–1866

Thomas Carleton   *1784–1817*
George Strachey Smyth   *1817–1823*
Sir Howard Douglas   *1824–1831*
Sir Archibald Campbell   *1831–1837*
Sir John Harvey   *1837–1841*
Sir William Colebrooke   *1841–1848*
Sir Edmund Head   *1848–1854*
Sir John Henry Manners-Sutton   *1854–1861*
Arthur Hamilton Gordon   *1861–1866*

Lieutenant Governors of Newfoundland 1789–1841

Mark Milbanke   *1789–1792*
Sir Richard King   *1792–1794*
Sir James Wallace   *1794–1797*
William Waldegrave   *1797–1800*
Sir Charles M. Pole   *1800–1801*
James Gambier   *1802–1804*
Sir Erasmus Gower   *1804–1806*
John Holloway   *1807–1809*
Sir John T. Duckworth   *1810–1813*
Sir Richard Godwin Keats   *1813–1816*
Sir Francis Pickmore   *1816–1818*
Sir Charles Hamilton   *1818–1824*
Sir Thomas John Cochrane   *1825–1834*
Henry Prescott   *1834–1841*

Lieutenant Governors of Nova Scotia (including Acadia) 1782–1867

John Parr   *1782–1791*
Sir John Wentworth   *1792–1808*

Sir George Provost   *1808–1811*
Sir John Sherbrooke   *1811–1816*
Earl of Dalhousie   *1816–1820*
Sir James Kempt   *1820–1828*
Sir Peregrine Maitland   *1828–1834*
Sir Colin Campbell   *1834–1840*
Lord Falkland   *1840–1846*
Sir John Harvey   *1846–1852*
Sir John LeMarchant   *1852–1858*
Earl of Mulgrave   *1858–1863*
Sir Richard MacDonnell   *1864–1865*
Sir W. Fenwick Williams   *1865–1867*

Lieutenant Governors of Ontatio 1792–1841

Colonel John Graves Simcoe   *1792–1796*
Peter Hunter   *1799–1805*
Francis Gore   *1806–1817*
Sir Peregrine Maitland   *1818–1828*
Sir John Colborne   *1828–1836*
Sir Francis Bond Head   *1836–1838*
Sir George Arthur   *1838–1841*

Lieutenant Governors of Prince Edward Island 1787–1873

Edmund Fanning   *1787–1805*
Joseph Frederick W. DesBarres   *1805–1812*
Charles D. Smith   *1813–1824*
John Ready   *1824–1831*
Sir Aretas Young   *1831–1835*
Sir John Harvey   *1836–1837*
Sir Charles Fitzroy   *1837–1841*
Sir Henry Vere Huntley   *1841–1847*
Sir Donald Campbell   *1847–1850*

Ambrose Lane   *1850–1851*
Sir Alexander Bannerman   *1851–*
   1854
Sir Dominique Daly   *1854–1859*
George Dundas   *1859–1868*
Sir Robert Hodgson   *1868–1870*
William C.F. Robinson   *1870–*
   1873

Premiers of Alberta from 1905

Alexander Cameron Rutherford	Liberal	*1905–1910*
Arthur Lewis Sifton	Liberal	*1910–1917*
Charles Stewart	Liberal	*1917–1921*
Herbert Greenfield	United Farmers of Alberta	*1921–1925*
John Edward Brownlee	United Farmers of Alberta	*1925–1934*
Richard Gavin Reid	United Farmers of Alberta	*1934–1935*
William Aberhart	Social Credit	*1935–1943*
Ernest Charles Manning	Social Credit	*1943–1968*
Harry Edwin Strom	Social Credit	*1968–1971*
Peter Lougheed	Conservative	*1971–1985*
Donald Ross Getty	Conservative	*1985–1992*
Ralph Klein	Conservative	*1992–Present*

Premiers of British Columbia from 1871

John Foster McCreight		*1871–1872*
Amor De Cosmos		*1872–1874*
George Anthony Walkem		*1874–1876*
Andrew Charles Elliott		*1878–1882*
Robert Beaven		*1882–1883*
William Smithe		*1883–1887*
Alexander Edmund Batson Davie	Conservative	*1887–1889*
John Robson	Liberal	*1889–1892*
Theodore Davie		*1892–1895*
John Herbert Turner		*1895–1898*
Charles Augustin Semlin	Conservative	*1898–1900*
Joseph Martin	Liberal	*1900*
James Dunsmuir	Conservative	*1900–1902*
Edward Gawler Prior	Conservative	*1902–1903*
Sir Richard McBride	Conservative	*1903–1915*
William John Bowser	Conservative	*1915–1916*
Harlan Carey Brewster	Liberal	*1916–1918*
John Oliver	Liberal	*1918–1927*
John Duncan MacLean	Liberal	*1927–1928*
Simon Fraser Tolmie	Conservative	*1928–1933*
Thomas Dufferin Pattullo	Liberal	*1933–1941*
John Hart	Coalition Govt	*1941–1947*
Byron Ingemar Johnson	Coalition Govt	*1947–1952*
William Andrew Cecil Bennett	Social Credit	*1952–1972*
David Barrett	NDP	*1972–1975*
William Richards Bennett	Social Credit	*1975–1986*
Bill Van Der Zalm	Social Credit	*1986–1991*
Rita Johnston	Social Credit	*1991*
Michael Harcourt	NDP	*1991–1996*
Glen Clark	NDP	*1996–1999*
Dan Miller	NDP	*1999–2000*
Ujjal Dosanjh	NDP	*2000–*

Premiers of Manitoba from 1870

Alfred Boyd	nonpartisan	*1870–1871*
Marc A. Girard	nonpartisan	*1871–1872*
Henry J. Clarke	nonpartisan	*1872–1874*
Marc A. Girard	nonpartisan	*1874*
Robert A. Davis	nonpartisan	*1874–1878*
John Norquay	nonpartisan	*1878–1887*
David H. Harrison	nonpartisan	*1887–1888*
Thomas Greenway	Liberal	*1888–1900*
Hugh John Macdonald	Conservative	*1900*
Rodmond P. Roblin	Conservative	*1900–1915*
Tobias C. Norris	Liberal	*1915–1922*
John Bracken	United Farmers of Manitoba	*1922–1928*
John Bracken	Coalition	*1928–1942*
Stuart S. Garson	Coalition	*1942–1948*
Douglas L. Campbell	Coalition	*1948–1958*
Dufferin Roblin	Conservative	*1958–1967*
Walter C. Weir	Conservative	*1967–1969*
Edward R. Schreyer	NDP	*1969–1977*
Sterling Lyon	Conservative	*1977–1981*
Howard Pawley	NDP	*1981–1988*
Garry Filmon	Conservative	*1988–Present*

Premiers of New Brunswick from 1866

Peter Mitchell		*1866–1867*
Andrew Rainsford Wetmore		*1867–1870*
George Luther Hatheway		*1871–1872*
George Edwin King	Conservative	*1872–1878*
John James Fraser		*1878–1882*
Daniel Lionel Hanington	Conservative	*1882–1883*
Andrew George Blair	Liberal	*1883–1896*
James Mitchell	Liberal	*1896–1897*
Henry Robert Emmerson	Liberal	*1897–1900*
Lemuel John Tweedle	Liberal	*1900–1907*
William Pugsley	Liberal	*1907*
Clifford William Robertson	Liberal	*1907–1908*
Sir John Douglas Hazen	Conservative	*1908–1911*
James Kidd Flemming	Conservative	*1911–1914*
George Johnson Clarke	Conservative	*1914–1917*
James Alexander Murray	Conservative	*1917*
Walter Edward Foster	Liberal	*1917–1923*
Peter John Veniot	Liberal	*1923–1925*
John Babington Macaulay Baxter	Conservative	*1925–1931*
Charles Dow Richards	Conservative	*1931–1933*
Leonard Percy de Wolfe Tilley	Conservative	*1933–1935*
A. Allison Dysart	Liberal	*1935–1940*
John Babbitt McNair	Liberal	*1940–1952*
Hugh John Flemming	Conservative	*1952–1960*
Louis J. Robichaud	Liberal	*1960–1970*
Richard B. Hatfield	Conservative	*1970–1987*
Frank McKenna	Liberal	*1987–1998*
Camille Thériault	Liberal	*1998-1999*
Bernard Lord	Conservative	*1999–Present*

Premiers of Nova Scotia from 1867

Hiram Blanchard	Liberal	1867
William Annand	Anti-Confederation	1867–1875
Philip Carteret Hill	Liberal	1875–1878
Simon Hugh Holmes	Conservative	1878–1882
Sir John Sparrow David Thompson	Conservative	1882
William Thomas Pipes	Liberal	1882–1884
William Stevens Fielding	Liberal	1884–1896
George Henry Murray	Liberal	1896–1923
Ernest Howard Armstrong	Liberal	1923–1925
Edgar Nelson Rhodes	Conservative	1925–1930
Gordon Sidney Harrington	Conservative	1930–1933
Angus Lewis Macdonald	Liberal	1933–1940
Alexander Sterling MacMillan	Liberal	1940–1945
Angus Lewis Macdonald	Liberal	1945–1954
Harold Joseph Connolly	Liberal	1954
Henry Davies Hicks	Liberal	1954–1956
Robert Lorne Stanfield	Conservative	1956–1967
George Isaac Smith	Conservative	1967–1970
Gerald A. Regan	Liberal	1970–1978
John MacLennan Buchanan	Conservative	1978–1990
Roger Stuart Bacon	Conservative	1990–1991
Donald William Cameron	Conservative	1991–1993
John Savage	Liberal	1993–1998
Russell MacLellan	Liberal	1998–1999
John Hamm	Conservative	1999–Present

Premiers of Newfoundland from 1949

Joseph R. Smallwood	Liberal	*1949–1972*
Frank D. Moores	Conservative	*1972–1979*
A. Brian Peckford	Conservative	*1979–1989*
Thomas Rideout	Conservative	*1989*
Clyde Wells	Liberal	*1989–1996*
Brian Tobin	Liberal	*1996–1999*
Beaton Tulk	Liberal	*2000–*

Premiers of Ontario from 1867

John Sandfield Macdonald	Liberal–Conservative	*1867–1871*
Edward Blake	Liberal	*1871–1872*
Oliver Mowat	Liberal	*1872–1896*
Arthur Sturgis Hardy	Liberal	*1896–1899*
George William Ross	Liberal	*1899–1905*
James Pliny Whitney	Conservative	*1905–1914*
William Howard Hearst	Conservative	*1914–1919*
Ernest Charles Drury	United Farmers of Ontario	*1919–1923*
George Howard Ferguson	Conservative	*1923–1930*
George Stewart Henry	Conservative	*1930–1934*
Mitchell Frederick Hepburn	Liberal	*1934–1942*
Gordon Daniel Conant	Liberal	*1942–1943*
Harry Corwin Nixon	Liberal	*1943*
George Alexander Drew	Conservative	*1943–1948*
Thomas Laird Kennedy	Conservative	*1948–1949*
Leslie Miscampbell Frost	Conservative	*1949–1961*
John Parmenter Robarts	Conservative	*1961–1971*
William Grenville Davis	Conservative	*1971–1985*
Frank Miller	Conservative	*1985*
David Robert Peterson	Liberal	*1985–1990*
Bob Rae	NDP	*1990–1995*
Mike Harris	Conservative	*1995–Present*

Premiers of Prince Edward Island from 1873

James C. Pope	Conservative	*1873*
L.C. Owen	Conservative	*1873–1876*
Sir L. H. Davies	Liberal	*1876–1879*
W. W. Sullivan	Conservative	*1879–1889*
N. McLeod	Conservative	*1889–1891*
F. Peters	Liberal	*1891–1897*
A. B. Warburton	Liberal	*1897–1898*
D. Farquharson	Liberal	*1898–1901*
A. Peters	Liberal	*1901–1908*
F. L. Haszard	Liberal	*1908–1911*
H. James Palmer	Liberal	*1911*
John A. Mathieson	Conservative	*1911–1917*
Aubin E. Arsenault	Conservative	*1917–1919*
J. H. Bell	Liberal	*1919–1923*
James D. Stewart	Conservative	*1923–1927*
Albert C. Saunders	Liberal	*1927–1930*
Walter M. Lea	Liberal	*1930–1931*
James D. Stewart	Conservative	*1931–1933*
William J. P. MacMillan	Conservative	*1933–1935*
Walter M. Lea	Liberal	*1935–1936*
Thane A. Campbell	Liberal	*1936–1943*
J. Walter Jones	Liberal	*1943–1953*
Alexander W. Matheson	Liberal	*1953–1959*
Walter R. Shaw	Conservative	*1959–1966*
Alexander B. Campbell	Liberal	*1966–1978*
W. Bennett Campbell	Liberal	*1978–1979*
J. Angus McLean	Conservative	*1979–1981*
James M. Lee	Conservative	*1981–1986*
James A. Ghiz	Liberal	*1986–1993*
Catherine Callbeck	Liberal	*1993–1996*
Patrick George Binns	Conservative	*1996–Present*

Premiers of Quebec from 1867

Pierre-Joseph-Olivier Chauveau	Conservative	*1867–1873*
Gédéon Ouimet	Conservative	*1873–1874*
Sir Charles-Eugène Boucher de Boucherville	Conservative	*1874–1878*
Sir Henri-Gustave Joly de Lotbinère	Liberal	*1878–1879*
Sir Joseph-Adolphe Chapleau	Conservative	*1879–1882*
Joseph-Alfred Mousseau	Conservative	*1882–1884*
John Jones Ross	Conservative	*1884–1887*
Louis-Olivier Taillon	Conservative	*1887*
Honoré Mercier	Liberal	*1887–1891*
Sir Charles-Eugène Boucher de Boucherville	Conservative	*1891–1892*
Sir Louis-Olivier Taillon	Conservative	*1892–1896*
Edmund James Flynn	Conservative	*1896–1897*
Félix-Gabriel Marchand	Liberal	*1897–1900*
Simon Napoléon Parent	Liberal	*1900–1905*
Sir Jean-Lomer Gouin	Liberal	*1905–1920*
Louis-Alexandre Taschereau	Liberal	*1920–1936*
Joseph-Adélard Godbout	Liberal	*1936*
Maurice Duplessis	Union Nationale	*1936–1939*
Joseph-Adélard Godbout	Liberal	*1939–1944*
Maurice Duplessis	Union Nationale	*1944–1959*
Paul Sauvé	Union Nationale	*1959–1960*
J. Antonio Barrette	Union Nationale	*1960*
Jean Lesage	Liberal	*1960–1966*
Daniel Johnson	Union Nationale	*1966–1968*
Jean-Jacques Bertrand	Union Nationale	*1968–1970*
Robert Bourassa	Liberal	*1970–1976*
René Lévesque	Parti Québécois	*1976–1985*
Pierre-Marc Johnson	Parti Québécois	*1985*
Robert Bourassa	Liberal	*1985–1994*

Daniel Johnson	Liberal	*1994*
Jacques Parizeau	Parti Québécois	*1994–1996*
Lucien Bouchard	Parti Québécois	*1996–Present*

Premiers of Saskatchewan from 1905

T. Walter Scott	Liberal	*1905–1916*
William M. Martin	Liberal	*1916–1922*
Charles A. Dunning	Liberal	*1922–1926*
James G. Gardiner	Liberal	*1926–1929*
James J. T. Anderson	Conservative	*1929–1934*
James G. Gardiner	Liberal	*1934–1935*
William J. Patterson	Liberal	*1935–1944*
Thomas C. Douglas	CCF / NDP	*1944–1961*
Woodrow S. Lloyd	CCF / NDP	*1961–1964*
W. Ross Thatcher	Liberal	*1964–1971*
Allan E. Blakeney	NDP	*1971–1982*
D. Grant Devine	Conservative	*1982–1991*
Roy Romanow	NDP	*1991–Present*

Prime Ministers of Canada from 1867

Sir John A. Macdonald   *1867–1873*
Alexander Mackenzie   *1873–1878*
Sir John A. Macdonald   *1878–1891*
Sir John Abbott   *1891–1892*
Sir John Thompson   *1892–1894*
Sir Mackenzie Bowell   *1894–1896*
Sir Charles Tupper   *1896*
Sir Wilfrid Laurier   *1896–1911*
Sir Robert Borden   *1911–1920*
Arthur Meighen   *1920–1921*
Mackenzie King   *1921–1926*
Arthur Meighen   *1926*
Mackenzie King   *1926–1930*

Richard Bedford Bennett   *1930–1935*
Mackenzie King   *1935–1948*
Louis St Laurent   *1948–1957*
John Diefenbaker   *1957–1963*
Lester B. Pearson   *1963–1968*
Pierre Elliott Trudeau   *1968–1979*
Joe Clark   *1979–1980*
Pierre Elliott Trudeau   *1980–1984*
John Turner   *1984*
Brian Mulroney   *1984–1993*
Kim Campbell   *1993*
Jean Chrétien   *1993–Present*

Chronology of Major Events

B.C.

14000   First certain human habitation in Canada.

A.D.

985	Bjarni Herjolfsen first sights North America on a voyage from Greenland.
990	Norse colony established at L'Anse-aux-Meadows, Newfoundland.
1480s	Fishing fleets from Western Europe reach the western Atlantic.
1497	John Cabot (Giovanni Caboto) claims Newfoundland for Henry VII of England.
1498	Cabot's second voyage reaches Nova Scotia.
1500	Gaspar Corte Real sails along the shores of northeastern North America.
1524	Verrazano maps northeast coast of North America.
1534	Jacques Cartier explores the Gulf of St Lawrence.
1535–36	Jacques Cartier ascends the St Lawrence River to Montreal and winters at Quebec.
1541–42	Jacques Cartier and Sieur de Roberval winter at Quebec.
1577	Martin Frobisher discovers Frobisher Bay on Baffin Island.
1608	Samuel de Champlain establishes a permanent colony at Quebec.
1610	Henry Hudson discovers Hudson Strait and Hudson Bay.
1629	Quebec is captured by the English; returned to France in 1632.
1635	Death of Champlain.
1642	Montreal founded by Sieur de Maisonneuve.
1649–50	Iroquois finally sweep away the Hurons and the Jesuits from Huronia.
1670	Founding of the Hudson's Bay Company.
1672–82	Comte de Frontenac, governor of New France.

1673	Fort Frontenac established on site of Kingston, Ontario.
1678	Father Louis Hennepin discovers Niagara Falls.
1682	Sieur de La Salle descends the Mississippi River to its mouth.
1683	York Factory established by Hudson's Bay Company.
1689	Iroquois raid on Lachine, outside Montreal.
1689–98	Frontenac's second term as governor of New France.
1690	British attack on Quebec fails.
1690–92	Henry Kelsey reaches Saskatchewan River from Hudson Bay.
1710	The British capture the Annapolis Valley.
1711	British naval expedition to capture Quebec fails.
1713	Treaty of Utrecht confirms British possession of Nova Scotia, Newfoundland and the Hudson's Bay lands.
1718	New Orleans founded by Sieur de Bienville.
1720–40	Fortress of Louisbourg, designed by Vauban, erected on Cape Breton Island.
1726	French build stone Fort Niagara.
1731–43	Sieur de la Vérendrye and sons open up the fur trade between New France and the Great Plains.
1738	Iron foundry established near Trois-Rivières.
1745	Louisbourg captured by an Anglo–American force.
1749	Halifax founded.
1756	French capture Fort Oswego.
1757	French capture Fort William Henry.
1758	Louisbourg in the east, Fort Ticonderoga in the centre and Fort Frontenac on Lake Ontario fall to the British. First meeting of the Nova Scotia legislature.
1759	British capture Fort Niagara and Quebec City.
1760	Montreal surrenders to the British.
1763	Treaty of Paris confirms the cession of New France to Great Britain.
1774	Quebec Act recognizes the use of the French language in the courts in Quebec.
1775	American rebels capture Montreal; American attack on Quebec City fails.
1776	Americans evacuate Montreal.
1777	British defeated by Americans at Saratoga.
1778	Americans ravage Iroquois lands.
1783	Treaty of Versailles confirms the independence of the United States and the retention of Quebec and Nova Scotia by the British.
1791	Constitutional Act divides Quebec into the provinces of Upper Canada and Lower Canada, and establishes legislatures in the two provinces.

1794	Lieutenant-Governor Simcoe makes York (now Toronto) capital of Upper Canada.
1812	Outbreak of war between Great Britain and the United States. American attacks on Canada repelled.
1813	Americans capture and burn York (UC); British capture Fort Niagara and burn Buffalo.
1814	British capture and burn Washington; peace concluded between Great Britain and the United States at Ghent; status quo of 1812 restored.
1821–25	Construction of Lachine Canal near Montreal.
1826–32	Construction of Rideau Canal between Ottawa River and Lake Ontario.
1830s	Increasing friction between British governors in Upper Canada and Lower Canada and the local legislatures.
1837	First Canadian railway.
1837–38	Rebellions in Upper Canada and Lower Canada suppressed by British Army and local militia.
1838	Earl of Durham sent to investigate conditions in British North America and to make recommendations. Durham Report urges empowering local legislatures.
1840	Act of Union unites Upper Canada and Lower Canada.
1848	Local control, 'responsible government,' achieved in provinces of Nova Scotia and Canada.
1859	Victoria Bridge completed spanning the St Lawrence at Montreal.
1860	Grand Trunk Railway completed from Sarnia to Rivière du Loup.
1864	Representatives of British provinces in North America meet at Charlottetown and Quebec to draw up a plan for the union of the colonies.
1867	Provinces of Canada, Nova Scotia and New Brunswick joined in the Dominion of Canada; provinces of Ontario and Quebec created; first federal election won by the Conservatives led by Prime Minister Sir John A. Macdonald.
1869–70	Red River Rebellion; admission of Manitoba as a province; Hudson's Bay Company lands (Rupert's Land) purchased by Canadian government.
1871	British Columbia joins Canada.
1872	Conservatives win second federal election.
1873	Prince Edward Island joins Canada; Pacific Scandal; Conservatives lose office; Liberals take power under Alexander Mackenzie.

1876	Intercolonial Railway completed from Halifax to Rivière du Loup.
1878	Federal elections return Sir John A. Macdonald and the Conservatives to office.
1879	Conservatives enact 'National Policy,' raising tariffs to new heights.
1880	British turn over Arctic islands to Canadian administration.
1883	Federal elections: Macdonald and Conservatives win again.
1885	Northwest Rebellion led by Louis Riel suppressed; Riel hanged; completion of Canadian Pacific Railway from Montreal to Vancouver.
1887	Federal elections: Macdonald and Conservatives win again.
1891	Federal elections on issue of reciprocity with United States; Macdonald and Conservatives win and reciprocity loses; death of Macdonald.
1896	Federal elections: Liberals under Wilfrid Laurier win.
1899	Canada sends troops to South African War.
1900	Federal elections: Laurier and Liberals win.
1903	Alaska Boundary dispute with United States arbitrated in the latter's favour.
1904	Federal elections: Laurier and Liberals win.
1905	Creation of provinces of Alberta and Saskatchewan.
1908	Federal elections: Laurier and Liberals win.
1909	Laurier establishes Department of External Affairs; Boundary Waters Treaty establishes International Joint Commission with United States.
1910	Laurier establishes Canadian Navy.
1911	Government signs reciprocity agreement with United States; in subsequent federal elections Liberals lose to Conservatives under Robert Borden.
1913	Borden's naval policy defeated in Senate.
1914	Outbreak of World War I; Canada sends army contingent to Europe.
1915	Canadians fight in Battle of Ypres.
1916	Manitoba becomes first province to give women the vote.
1916	Newfoundland Regiment decimated in Battle of Beaumont–Hamel.
1917	Canadians take Vimy Ridge; coalition government formed in Ottawa to implement conscription; in subsequent federal elections, Conservatives and conscriptionist Liberals defeat Laurier.
1918	Canadian army participates in victorious Allied offensive in France; Germany granted an armistice.

1919	Canada signs Treaty of Versailles; general strike in Winnipeg.
1920	Arthur Meighen succeeds Borden as prime minister.
1921	In federal elections, Liberals under Mackenzie King defeat Meighen government.
1923	Canada signs Halibut Treaty with United States: first treaty without British participation.
1925	Liberals secure minority government in federal elections.
1926	Liberal government is defeated in Parliament; Mackenzie King is succeeded by Arthur Meighen, whose government is in turn defeated by Liberals under King in a general election; King returns as prime minister.
1927	Federal-provincial conference first considers amending the Canadian constitution in Canada, with no result.
1928–9	Fall in commodity prices heralds the Great Depression.
1930	R. B. Bennett and the Conservative Party defeat the Liberals in general elections; Bennett becomes prime minister.
1931	Statute of Westminster ratifies Canadian autonomy from British legislation – except for the amendment of the constitution.
1932	Ottawa Conference establishes system of Imperial Preference in the British Empire; riots in Newfoundland topple government, which is replaced by a British-appointed commission.
1933	Lowest point of the Great Depression in Canada – 50% of 1928 GDP.
1935	Mackenzie King becomes prime minister again after defeating R. B. Bennett in a general election.
1936	Government establishes Canadian Broadcasting Commission (CBC).
1937	Government establishes Trans-Canada Airlines, later Air Canada.
1939	Canada declares war on Nazi Germany on September 10.
1940	King government is confirmed in power by a general election; in June, Parliament enacts conscription for home defence.
1941	A constitutional amendment gives power over unemployment insurance to the federal government.
1942	Canadian Army takes part in disastrous Dieppe Raid.
1943	Canadian troops participate in the invasions of Sicily and Italy.
1944	Canadian troops land in Normandy and participate in the battle for Northwest Europe; conscripts sent to Europe.
1945	Canadian army liberates the Netherlands.
1945	King and the Liberals win a narrow majority in a general election; Canada becomes a founding member of the United Nations (UN).

1947	Citizenship Act establishes separate Canadian citizenship. Canada joins the General Agreement on Tariffs and Trade (GATT).
1948	King retires as prime minister and is succeeded by Louis St Laurent.
1949	Newfoundland becomes Canada's tenth province. Canada becomes a founding member of North Atlantic Treaty Organisation (NATO); St Laurent and the Liberals win an increased majority in a general election.
1950	Canada sends armed forces to support UN intervention in Korea.
1951	Canadian army and air force return to Europe as part of NATO garrison.
1953	Korean War ends; St. Laurent and the Liberals win another majority in a general election.
1957	Progressive Conservatives under John Diefenbaker narrowly defeat the Liberals and form a minority government.
1958	Lester B. Pearson becomes Liberal leader; Diefenbaker and the Progressive Conservatives win a smashing victory in a general election.
1959	Government cancels development of the supersonic fighter, the Avro Arrow.
1960	Jean Lesage and the Liberal Party win general election in Quebec; 'Quiet Revolution' in Quebec begins.
1962	Diefenbaker government loses majority in a general election.
1963	Diefenbaker government is defeated in Parliament and then in a general election; Pearson and the Liberals form a minority government; terrorist incidents begin in Quebec.
1965	Pearson calls a snap general election but wins only a second minority government.
1967	France's President Charles de Gaulle visits Canadian centennial celebrations and calls for a 'free Quebec;' Diefenbaker is retired as Conservative leader.
1968	Liberal convention chooses justice minister Pierre Trudeau to replace Lester Pearson as party leader. Prime Minister Trudeau and the Liberals win a majority in a general election.
1970	Terrorists kidnap Quebec labour minister and British consul, murdering the former; Trudeau calls in the army and proclaims a state of 'apprehended insurrection' in Quebec; terrorism subsides.
1972	In a general election, Trudeau retains a plurality of two seats in Parliament.
1973	Oil crisis begins; inflation and unemployment rise.

1974	Trudeau, outmanoeuvring the opposition, calls an early general election, in which he and the Liberals win a majority.
1975	The federal government imposes wage and price controls.
1976	The separatist Parti Québécois wins an election in Quebec and forms a government.
1979	The Progressive Conservatives under Joe Clark narrowly defeat the Liberals; Clark becomes prime minister of a minority government; in December, Clark's government is defeated in Parliament.
1980	Trudeau and the Liberals win another general election and form a majority government; the Quebec government calls and loses a referendum on Quebec separation; government formulates a 'National Energy Program'.
1981	Trudeau secures agreement from nine provinces, except Quebec, on amending the constitution within Canada and on a Charter of Rights and Freedoms; Trudeau's initiative is sustained by the courts.
1981–82	Deep but short-lived economic recession.
1982	Queen Elizabeth II signs new constitution into law.
1983	Government seeks sectoral free trade with the United States; Joe Clark is replaced as Conservative leader by Brian Mulroney.
1984	Trudeau retires and is succeeded as Liberal leader and prime minister by John Turner; Turner loses a general election to Brian Mulroney and the Progressive Conservatives, who form a majority government.
1985	Mulroney begins negotiations for a free trade agreement with the United States; separatist government in Quebec replaced by Liberals under Robert Bourassa.
1987	Free Trade Agreement is signed with the United States; Mulroney and the provincial premiers agree on a package of constitutional reforms at Meech Lake.
1988	Liberals obstruct ratification of the Free Trade Agreement and force a general election, which they lose.
1989	Free Trade Agreement enters into force.
1990	Mulroney's Meech Lake constitutional reforms fail to be ratified; separatism rises in Quebec.
1991–92	A sharp economic recession deepens the government's unpopularity; unemployment remains high throughout the decade.
1992	A second set of constitutional reforms is defeated in a national referendum.
1993	Mulroney retires as prime minister and is succeeded by Kim

	Campbell, who calls and loses a general election; Jean Chrétien and the Liberals form a majority government; the Conservative Party is almost obliterated in the election.
1994	The separatists win a general election in Quebec and form a government.
1995	In a referendum on Quebec sovereignty, the separatists narrowly lose.
1997	Chrétien and the Liberals win a second majority government in a general election.
1998	Separatists win a second term in a Quebec provincial election.
1999–2000	Chrétien government introduces and passes a 'Clarity Act' defining how a province may secede from the Canadian federation.
2000	A new opposition party, the right-wing Canadian Alliance, is founded by dissident Conservatives and the Reform Party.
2000	Chrétien's Liberal government wins a third straight majority in a national general election.

Further Reading

General

The single best source on Canada is *The Canadian Encyclopedia*, available in both print and CD-ROM format: Toronto, McClelland & Stewart, latest edition 1999. It is infinitely superior to the government's *Canada Year Book*, which presents a collage of pretty pictures, politically correct text, and sparse statistics. The best single volume history is *The Illustrated History of Canada*, edited by R. Craig Brown (Toronto, Key Porter, 2000).

BEFORE 1760

ANDERSON, FRED *Crucible of War: the Seven Years' War and the Fate of Empire in British North America, 1754–1766* (New York: Knopf, 2000)

DICKASON, OLIVE *Canada's First Nations: a History of Founding Peoples from Earliest Times* (Toronto: OUP, 1992)

ECCLES, WILLIAM J. *Canada under Louis XIV, 1663–1701* (Toronto: McClelland and Stewart, 1964)

– – –. *The Canadian Frontier, 1534–1760*, rev. ed. (Albuquerque: U of New Mexico Press, 1983)

– – –. *Canadian Society during the French Regime* (Montreal: Harvest House, 1968)

– – –. *The French in North America, 1500–1783*, rev. ed. (Markham, Ont.: Fitzhenry and Whiteside, 1998)

GREER, ALLAN *The People of New France* (Toronto: U of Toronto Press, 1997)

MILLER, JAMES R. *Skyscrapers Hide the Heavens* (Toronto: U of Toronto Press, 1991)

WRIGHT, J.V. *A History of the Native People of Canada* (Hull, Que. Canadian Museum of Civilization, 1995)

THE BRITISH REGIME, 1760–1867

CARELESS, J.M.S. *The Union of the Canadas: the Growth of Canadian Institutions, 1841–1857* (Toronto: McClelland and Stewart, 1967)

CRAIG, GERALD *Upper Canada: the Formative Years, 1784–1841* (Toronto: McClelland and Stewart, 1963)

FRIESEN, GERALD *The Canadian Prairies: a History* (Toronto: U of Toronto Press, 1984)

GREER, ALLAN *The Patriots and the People: the Rebellion of 1837 in Rural Lower Canada* (Toronto: U of Toronto Press, 1993)

– – –. *Peasant, Lord, and Merchant: Rural society in Three Quebec Parishes, 1740–1840* (Toronto: U of Toronto Press, 1985)

MORTON, W.L. *The Critical Years: the Union of British North America, 1857–1873* (Toronto: McClelland and Stewart, 1964)

ORMSBY, MARGARET *British Columbia, a History* (Toronto: Macmillan, 1958)

TROFIMENKOFF, SUSAN *The Dream of Nation: a social and intellectual history of Quebec* (Toronto: Gage, 1983)

1867–1945

BOTHWELL, ROBERT, DRUMMOND, IAN, and ENGLISH, JOHN *Canada 1900–1945* (Toronto: U of Toronto Press, 1987)

BROWN, R. CRAIG and COOK, RAMSAY *Canada 1896–1921* (Toronto: McClelland & Stewart, 1974)

DUROCHER, RENÉ, LINTEAU, PAUL-ANDRÉ and ROBERT, JEAN-CLAUDE *Histoire du Québec contemporain*, 2 vols, new ed. (Montréal: Boréal Express, 1989) OR *Quebec, a History 1867–1929*, trans. Robert Chodos (Toronto: J. Lorimer, 1983)

NORRIE, KENNETH and OWRAM, DOUG *A History of the Canadian Economy* (Toronto: Harcourt Brace Jovanovich, 1991)

STACEY, CHARLES P. *Canada and the Age of Conflict*, 2 vols. (Toronto: University of Toronto Press, 1984)

1945–2000

BOTHWELL, ROBERT, DRUMMOND, IAN, and ENGLISH, JOHN *Canada since 1945* (Toronto: U of Toronto Press, 2nd ed., 1988)

BOTHWELL, ROBERT *Canada and the United States* (New York: Twayne, 1992)

Historical Gazetteer

Numbers in bold refer to main text

ALBERTA

Calgary and Banff Sited on the Bow River in the foothills of the **Rocky Mountains** (plainly visible from the city), Calgary is the centre of the Canadian oil industry and is second to Toronto in numbers of corporate head offices.

The Blackfoot, Stony and Sarcee originally inhabited the Calgary region. White explorers penetrated the area in the late 18th century, but there was no permanent white settlement until the North-West Mounted Police established Fort Calgary in 1875. The Canadian Pacific Railway reached the fort in 1883, foreshadowing Calgary's position as the dominant transportation centre for the southwest Great Plains and eastern British Columbia. Calgary grew in population, becoming a city in 1893; it failed, however, to

Spirit Island, Alberta

become the capital of the new province of Alberta in 1905 and thereafter cherished a rivalry with Edmonton, the actual capital. Calgary was a ranching and farming centre in the early 20th century, but it was the discovery of oil in 1947 that really set the city on the road to prosperity.

West of Calgary the Trans-Canada Highway climbs toward Banff National Park in the Rockies. The site of a railway hotel and a hot spring, with surrounding town, Banff perches uneasily between development for a much-enlarged tourism industry and the preservation of its beautiful mountain environment. The icefields north of Banff on the road to Jasper are particularly spectacular. **111**

Edmonton North of Calgary lies Edmonton, the provincial capital, a city of almost equal population. Edmonton does not have the Rockies, but it does have the deep valley of the North Saskatchewan River, which gives its riverside areas a certain scenic grandeur. Edmonton is the jumping-off point for the north and northwest, by road, rail or, especially, air. **80**

BRITISH COLUMBIA

Victoria and Vancouver Island Victoria is situated on a natural harbour at the southern tip of Vancouver Island. Originally Fort Victoria, a fur-trading post, it became first the capital of the colony of Vancouver Island and then the capital of the colony, later province, of British Columbia. The

presence of government is evident in Victoria (one of the main thoroughfares is called Government Street). The provincial legislature sits close to the harbour, across from the British Columbia Museum. The Empress Hotel (named after Queen Victoria) dominates the other side of the harbour and recalls the days when adjacent Esquimalt was a Royal Navy base (until 1906). A naval base it remains, for the Canadian navy. A large retired population, attracted by Victoria's mild climate, characterizes the place and contributes to a somewhat sedate atmosphere.

North from Victoria a well-built highway stretches to the top of the island, via Nanaimo and Campbell River, past the various Gulf Islands; a branch snakes west through the mountains to the spectacular beaches of the Pacific Rim National Park near Tofino. The BC Ferries, a government agency, make it possible to reach even more remote points, such as Alert Bay, a Kwakiutl town with a notable museum and 'great house' used for ceremonial events and gatherings. **61, 77**

Vancouver and the Lower Mainland
Vancouver is Canada's major West Coast port, located on Burrard Inlet, a great natural harbour near the mouth of the Fraser River.

Named after Captain George Vancouver, who explored the seacoast in 1792, Vancouver was not actually settled until the 1860s. It owed its development to transport – its harbour and its location as the western terminus of Canada's first transcontinental railway, the Canadian Pacific. Vancouver was also located beside the Fraser Delta, a rich farming area.

The city was the scene of racial and social conflict for much of its history, until the 1940s: fear of Asian immigrants stimulated the one and a highly polarized economic and political system fed the other. More liberal attitudes after 1945 finally made overt racism unfashionable and Vancouver since the 1960s has been characterized by a heavy immigration from China and especially Hong Kong. Vancouver's politics, like those of British Columbia as a whole, alternate between poles of right and left, with little room for what elsewhere in Canada would be a majority centre. The distinction may in part be cultural: British Columbians refer to their province as 'lotus land,' said to be characterized by a more relaxed lifestyle, different from that of the overstressed east. There is also a sense of regional grievance based on distance if not remoteness from the rest of Canada; this grievance was expressed in the 1990s by support for the right-wing Reform Party that promised to alter the Canadian political system so as better to reflect Canada's regional nature.

The city lies in sight of the mountains of Washington State to the south and the Whistler ski resort to the north. Vancouver is a city of gardens, some on public land, like the campus of the University of British Columbia at the western end of the city, or Stanley Park downtown. There are the usual large towers (such

as the BC Hydro Building) and apartment buildings in the centre of the city, but Vancouver's charm lies in its beautiful residential areas, and in its cafés and bistros. The University of British Columbia has perhaps the best site in the city, though its architecture, as on most Canadian campuses, is not especially distinguished. Simon Fraser University, in Burnaby to the east of the city, sits on a mountain. Its main buildings, designed by Arthur Erickson (1963–65) focus on a central mall. **153**

MANITOBA AND SASKATCHEWAN

The huge central provinces of Manitoba and Saskatchewan are usually thought to be agricultural, flat and fertile. Most of their territory, however, belongs to the rocky **Canadian Shield** – a land of lakes, rivers and bogs. **1–4, 5–6** As a result, from the earliest times two distinct cultures existed in this part of the Canadian west before the coming of whites: woodland in the north (Cree) and plains (Blackfoot, Sioux, Assiniboine) in the south. The arrival of horses from the south, and of whites from the east and northeast altered the nature of life on the prairies. Fur traders soon linked the rivers and plains to the Great Lakes trading system, heading toward Montreal, or to Hudson Bay and the Hudson's Bay Company posts along the bay coast. Traders often settled down and took wives, formally or informally; as a result a new people, Métis, grew up, half Indian and half white, sometimes following the customs and practices of both their ancestral groups.

The first formal settlement, by a mixture of Métis and whites, occurred in the early 19th century around Fort Garry, on the Red River, on the site of modern Winnipeg (some of the buildings still exist). The Riel Rebellion of 1869–70 arose from uneasiness and ill will between layers of settlers in the colony, as well as the feebleness of administration by the Hudson's Bay Company. A compromise agreement created a new province, Manitoba, centred on Red River, and with Fort Garry, renamed Winnipeg, as its capital. **1–6**

Winnipeg became the transportation hub of western Canada. Because of the location of the great lakes of central Manitoba (Lakes Winnipeg, Winnipegosis and Manitoba) all land transport had to pass through or near Winnipeg. First the Canadian Pacific and then other transcontinental railways passed through, while dropping off trainloads of immigrants. Light manufacturing and railway shops gave Winnipeg a working class as well as an immigrant character, and it became a city deeply divided between the immigrant, working-class (and largely Jewish) north end and the bourgeois south end. In the 20th century, after the completion of the Panama Canal and the catastrophe of the Great Depression, Winnipeg's prospects faded. Other cities, further west, took on the role of distribution and transport centres, and Manitoba did not have the oil reserves that gave Alberta its boom times in the 1960s and 1970s.

Nevertheless, and in reaction to its adverse climate, Winnipeg has maintained a lively cultural life, notable for its theatre and the Royal Winnipeg Ballet. The Pulitzer Prize-winning novelist Carol Shields lived in the city for many years and Winnipeg is the setting of much of her work. Its neighbourhoods continue distinctive, and the city is grudgingly admired, especially by its thousands of expatriates. **83**

Saskatchewan too was a creation of the pre-World War I wheat boom. At one time Saskatchewan had the largest population on the plains, the third-largest in Canada. But the rapid settlement of the west in the 1900s was deceptive in more ways than one. First, the wheat economy was subject to a boom-and-bust cycle of international prices, far beyond the control of Canadian wheat farmers or the Canadian government. Second, the high times of the 1900s encouraged settlement of marginal land – the woodlands in the north, but especially the plains of the south. In good years, this did not matter – there could be years in a row with abundant rainfall. But sometimes the rains stopped, as they did in the 1930s, and the soil, and with the soil the farms and hopes of thousands, blew away. Black clouds could be seen as far away as Winnipeg. Combined with low prices for wheat, the 1930s spelled ruin for much of the prairie economy, and severely and permanently limited Saskatchewan's prospects.

Perhaps as a consequence of its adverse economic experiences, the province turned to democratic socialism in the 1940s, pioneering hospital insurance, health insurance and a variety of other social programmes. Not everyone liked the experiment, and as a result Saskatchewan politics have tended to be polarized between right and left. Along with the rest of Canada, Saskatchewan became urbanized in the 1960s and 1970s, and its two largest cities, **Regina** (the provincial capital) and **Saskatoon**, took on a larger role in provincial society and politics. Gradually rural towns and villages, with their characteristic grain elevators, declined (some disappeared altogether). Nevertheless, and despite the rise of a mining industry and light manufacturing, the provincial economy remained subject to booms and busts, especially as wheat prices declined in the late 1990s. In 1999-2000 a severe recession in agriculture darkened prospects for rural Saskatchewan, while leaving the urban areas largely unscathed.

Saskatchewan's two main cities are a surprise to the visitor, who frequently expects housing boxes on a succession of dusty rectangles. Saskatoon is dominated by the valley of the Saskatchewan River, with the nearby University of Saskatchewan providing a leafy refuge from summer heat. The university, the province's oldest, has tended to influence the culture of the city, which has also benefited economically from its links to the prospering mining industries of the north. Regina faced more of a challenge from geography than did Saskatoon. Sitting on the plains in the comparatively arid south of the province, Regina had to struggle to overcome its origins as a shack town known as 'Pile of Bones.' (The bones were those of the vanished buffalo, hunted almost to extinction in the 1870s and 1880s.) The settlement was renamed after the dignified Queen (Regina) Victoria and, when it became the provincial capital in 1905, undertook to compensate for its location by constructing an artificial lake, named Wascana, in 1912. The lake still exists, surrounded by beautiful parkland. Because of the presence of government, Regina has become something of a financial centre, and in addition to the provincial legislative buildings (which resemble those in US states, as do those in Alberta and Manitoba, in their neoclassical architecture) it has several mini-skyscrapers downtown. **5, 74, 75, 88–90, 153**

MARITIME PROVINCES
The provinces of **Prince Edward Island** and **New Brunswick**, and the adjacent Quebec region of Gaspé, stretch along the Gulf of St. Lawrence. Gaspé and New Brunswick are hilly and heavily forested and support a large forest industry.

Algonkian tribes originally settled the maritime region of Canada and remain to this day, especially the Micmac and the Malecite. They took sides in the Anglo-French wars of the 17th and 18th centuries, as French settlers and troops (resident since the early 17th century) struggled to defend their colony of Acadia against the British. The British, with seapower on their side, prevailed, though not without deporting, in 1755, as many of the Acadian population as they could get their hands on. Settlers from New England replaced the Acadians in the fertile Annapolis Valley and the St John Valley, while English, Scots and German settlers descended elsewhere. The Treaty of Paris of 1763 finally confirmed the region, called the province of Nova Scotia, as a British possession.

The Revolutionary War (1775–83) stirred the New England settlers in Nova Scotia but, separated from the other colonies by the British fleet and overawed by a British garrison, they remained quiet. Other Americans, loyal ones this time, arrived from Charleston and New York in 1782 and 1783 and quickly became the dominant force in this remaining British territory. To accommodate these United Empire Loyalists, the British created the province of New Brunswick in 1784 (Prince Edward Island had already been made a separate colony in 1769).

Meanwhile, Acadians who had escaped the British in 1755 and French Canadians from further west, in Quebec, filtered back, establishing settlements along the shore of the Gulf of St Lawrence from Gaspé to Cape Breton. These new (and sometimes old) Acadians coexisted generally peacefully with their English- and Gaelic-speaking neighbours; in New Brunswick they came to dominate most of the Atlantic Coast, effectively dividing the province into two cultural and linguistic zones. The English speakers centred on the provincial capital, Fredericton, and the largest port, Saint John, while

French speakers centred on Moncton. **32, 34, 43, 44, 53, 58, 75, 139**

Fredericton, on the St John River, enjoys a beautiful river frontage with a number of New England-style houses dating from the early 19th century. Because the city has been the provincial capital since the 18th century, government, in the form of a former British army barracks, the provincial legislature and the Anglican cathedral (dating from the time when the Church of England was the established church), is a prominent presence.

Life in **New Brunswick** was dominated by two factors: the sea and the forests. Exploitation of the forests and shipbuilding became the dominant industries of the 19th century, until the advent of iron and steam phased out wooden ships. Forests remain a large part of the provincial economy even in the 21st century. The St John River valley was a ribbon of fertility through the forests, and its soil and capabilities gave rise to a number of very large agri-businesses in the late 20th century. **32, 34, 43–44, 53, 58, 68, 69**

Prince Edward Island Prince Edward Island is a garden: flat farming and fishing country projecting into the sea. The island had for many years a peculiar system of absent landlords; as a consequence questions of land tenure dominated provincial politics in the 19th century. After the island joined Canada in 1873, emigration became one of the province's characteristics: its small size and limited opportunities guaranteed that most of its younger population would leave or at least seriously consider doing so. Only in the late 20th century did Prince Edward Island achieve the population it had had 100 years earlier. Remote, fertile and picturesque, Prince Edward Island became the stuff of romance – the 'Anne of Green Gables' series by the author Lucy Maud Montgomery was set there, affording Prince Edward Island an apparently perpetual popularity, especially among her many thousands of Japanese fans. The provincial capital, Charlottetown, named after the wife of George III, has a charming downtown, including a 19th-century provincial legislature. **32, 53, 58, 75**

Cape Breton Island Cape Breton Island, at the entrance to the Gulf of St Lawrence, is a land of contrasts. Hills, inlets and a large saltwater lake, Bras d'Or, give it some of the most spectacular scenery in Canada. It is also home to a declining industrial economy, formerly based on coal and steel, which despite repeated and very costly attempts at rejuvenation was by 2000 essentially moribund.

Cape Breton was first discovered by Basque fishermen and later settled by French immigrants. France retained the island under the Treaty of Utrecht of 1713, when the rest of Nova Scotia was ceded to the British. France at vast cost began construction of a town and stone fortress at **Louisbourg** on the Atlantic Coast. The town flourished as a seaport and garrison but had one fatal flaw: the surrounding hills commanded the fortifications. A British army took

Louisbourg in 1745 and again in 1758, after which the British blew up the fortifications. In 1961 the Canadian government began restoration of the old fort, which became a model of historical reconstruction.

The people of Cape Breton reflect the successive layers of settlement – French, spoken in some fishing villages, Scottish Gaelic, brought in the 18th century by highland settlers, but now almost extinct, and English. The folk traditions of Cape Breton gave rise to a flourishing musical revival in the 1990s that offset symbolically the island's economic decline. **22, 26, 32**

Halifax and Region Established on the natural harbour of Bedford Basin in 1749 by Colonel Edward Cornwallis, Halifax was originally intended as a focus for British settlement in Nova Scotia in opposition to French settlements on Cape Breton Island and the Annapolis Valley. In recognition of this role it became the capital of the province, whose first legislature met there in 1758. Cornwallis laid out the city on a grid plan, with the ocean on three sides and a military fortress on the other; the Citadel continues to dominate downtown Halifax.

At first threatened by neighbouring Indian tribes, Halifax after the 1760s was defended by its isolated location both by land and sea, and so it remained a centre of British naval power during the American Revolution and the later War of 1812. Indeed, Halifax remained a British naval base and army garrison until 1906, and defined its character in

The Clock Tower in Halifax

terms of a British and Anglican establishment. In the 19th century Halifax became a shipping, banking and mercantile centre, and by the mid-19th century a minor railway and manufacturing centre as well. After Nova Scotia became a province of Canada in 1867, Halifax became the Atlantic terminus for what eventually became the Canadian National Railway. In both World War I and World War II, Halifax became a major base for the Royal Canadian Navy and the principal point of departure for transatlantic convoys. In 1917 the explosion of a French munitions ship devastated the city. Over time, Halifax's excellent harbour and its function as a local distribution and service centre have guaranteed a certain continuity of prosperity. Nevertheless, its isolation on the far side of the Nova Scotian peninsula from the rest of eastern North America has meant that it has lost ground to more accessible ports on the American East Coast. City landmarks include the star-shaped Citadel (latest version 1825–56), St. Paul's Anglican Church (1750), Government House (1800) and Province House (1818). The Public Gardens resemble those in Boston. **31, 32, 34, 35, 40, 58, 80**

Newfoundland The island of Newfoundland was first discovered in the 990s by Norse explorers operating from Greenland and Iceland, and was briefly settled, on its northern tip at l'Anse-aux-Meadows. Many scholars identify the site as the Vinland of

Norse sagas, but whatever the truth of that assertion, it is beyond doubt that the Norse inhabited the place.

Newfoundland was rediscovered in 1497 by the explorer John Cabot, and claimed for Henry VII of England. The French disputed Newfoundland's ownership for many years, until the Treaty of Utrecht of 1713 gave it to Great Britain. The long imperial wars inhibited but did not obliterate settlement along the coasts, where fishermen and their families gradually settled, and Newfoundland remained the centre of a vast trade in fish, based on the cod of the Grand Banks, to the south of the island.

Newfoundland received the rudiments of government fairly late: in the 18th century the government was a British naval captain who came with the fishing fleet and left with it. Gradually, however, magistrates and more settled administration appeared. An elected provincial assembly was created in 1832, and responsible government (local responsibility) was conceded in 1855. Politics in Newfoundland were characterized by quarrels between Protestant and Catholic, English and Irish, St John's against the rest of the island, and merchants against fishermen.

The island stoutly refused to join Canada in 1867, and retained its autonomy for 80 years thereafter. Governments attempted to make ends meet by inviting investors (from Great Britain or from Canada) to exploit the island's resources. The result was the encouragement of a pulp and paper industry, iron mining, and a trans-island narrow-gauge rail-

way. The island was successful in asserting its claim to **Labrador**, a vast region on the mainland; but Labrador remained isolated and its resources awaited a new and more advanced technology before they could be reached. Nevertheless, Newfoundland remained poor and isolated, subject to the boom-and-bust cycle characteristic of primary products. The collapse of primary prices during the Great Depression of the 1930s actually led to the imminent bankruptcy of the Newfoundland government. To save the credit of the British Empire, the British government agreed to support Newfoundland; in return Newfoundland gave up its autonomous government and abolished its assembly in 1934. For the next 15 years Newfoundland was governed by British civil servants, until, after two referendums, the voters narrowly chose to join Canada in 1949.

Newfoundland's first premier after joining Canada, the charismatic Joey Smallwood, continued the tradition of encouraging resource exploitation. He also changed the face of the province, or at least the distribution of its population, by promoting the concentration of settlement, away from small fishing villages into larger centres. By joining Canada, Newfoundlanders got the benefits of the Canadian welfare state, but while this doubtless eased the poverty of the population, it did little to encourage a more viable and less dependent economy. Smallwood, desperate to convert water power in Labrador into saleable electricity, also signed a controversial contract with Quebec, through whose territory electricity lines would have to run on their way to markets in the United States. A huge hydro project at Churchill Falls was consequently built, but over the years Quebec collected most of the profit – a point of bitter contention for 30 years. In the 1980s and after there was hope of offshore oil (the Hibernia project) but there too profit seemed to be indefinitely postponed.

Newfoundland still retains traces of a distinctive accent, a blend of the speech of its two main immigrant groups, West Country English and Irish, although as elsewhere in North America the accent is gradually being homogenized into a continental norm. The island is a study in contrasts. The Avalon Peninsula, the first part of the island to be settled, centres on the provincial capital of St John's. Over many years, the peninsula has been denuded of trees, while the rest of the island remains heavily wooded. The eastern section of the Trans-Canada Highway crosses the province from St John's to a car ferry at Port-aux-Basques in the southwest. Around the province's coastline, and up to Labrador, there are supply boats that sometimes carry passengers and tourists to see what is probably the most remote part of North America, south of the Arctic. **9, 10, 11, 14, 26, 32–33, 45, 53, 58–59, 101, 151**

ONTARIO

Toronto and Region Situated on a rising plain on the north shore of Lake Ontario, Toronto is Canada's largest city and the country's banking and commercial centre. Toronto early became a trans-shipment point between Lake Ontario and Lake Simcoe and Georgian Bay, while its natural harbour, enclosed by a peninsula (converted into islands by a storm in 1858) attracted the attention of an early lieutenant-governor, John Graves Simcoe. In 1794 Simcoe decided to make the site, initially called York, the military and administrative centre of the province of Upper Canada. He erected Fort York near the lakeshore, and a legislative building some miles away. York grew very slowly to a mere 700 inhabitants in 1812, but as a provincial capital it attracted the attention of the Americans in the War of 1812. In April 1813 the US army raided the village, burned the legislature and other public buildings, and accidentally blew up Fort York, and their own commander. Postwar immigration hastened York's recovery, so that it reached a population of 9,000 in 1834 and became a city, named Toronto (probably meaning 'place of meeting,' in the Ojibway language). As Upper Canada's governmental centre, Toronto naturally had an advantage, as early banks clustered around government and the British garrison spent money in the locality. Steamboats made the city a regular port of call, followed by railways strung along the lakeshore in the 1850s. Light manufacturing and commerce flourished as Toronto's transportation connections made it the natural centre for the entire southern Ontario peninsula from Kingston in the east to Windsor

The waterfront in Toronto in the 1970s

in the west, with ongoing connections to Chicago and Detroit. Government continued to dominate: in 1867 Toronto became the provincial capital of Ontario and most important government functions, including the provincial university (the University of Toronto), were located there. Toronto in the late 19th century became a financial centre and railway centre and through its stock exchange dominated the Canadian mining industry. The mansion of one of the capitalists of the period, Sir Henry Pellatt, was so magnificently grandiose that it has been lovingly preserved under its original name, Casa Loma. Pellatt and his generation are also represented in a couple of bank head offices downtown, particularly the lavish Bank of Commerce building (1929–31) on King Street.

A later generation of business is represented in the bank towers of the 1960s and after, one for each major Canadian bank. These sit atop an ingenious underground maze of shops and walkways, modelled after Montreal's slightly earlier version. A telecommunications complex in the form of the very tall (1,815 feet) CN Tower dominates the downtown and is visible from most parts of the city. Beside the tower is the circular (and very expensive) Sky Dome with its retractable roof, home to Toronto's baseball team, the Blue Jays. Unlike the rival Olympic Stadium in Montreal, the roof actually functions.

Well into the 20th century, Toronto remained a homogeneous, English-speaking and British-derived city, where even Catholics were a small minority. Toronto's (and Ontario's) restrictions on public amusements and even necessities were notorious: Sunday activity of any kind was only gradually and reluctantly conceded (sports and movies in the 1950s, Sunday shopping in the 1990s). Parts of the city banned the sale of alcohol up until the 1990s. The ethnic mix changed after

World War II, as first immigration from southern Europe and then Asia and the West Indies changed the character of the city. By the 1970s Toronto was well known for its ethnic mix and while the city experienced stresses and strains as a result of the rapid influx and juxtaposition of ethnic groups, there were no serious riots as in American cities at the same time. Downtown residential areas in the 1970s and 1980s experienced an influx of young middle-class people, preserving the domestic character of neighbourhoods such as Rosedale or Cabbagetown. In the 1990s affluent housing spread, via a condominium craze, into parts of the downtown city previously reserved for the port (by then largely defunct) and factories.

Physically the city expanded from its original location around the harbour into its surrounding, previously rural, townships. In the 1950s the province forced a federation of Toronto with neighbouring and formerly rural municipalities, creating a metropolitan system, and then in 1998 amalgamated the municipalities into a single city of Toronto. The city government expanded apace, from a late Victorian edifice (still extant) to a soaring semicircular building designed by the Finnish architect, Viljo Revell, in the 1960s. An odd feature of the post-amalgamation city is the existence of two would-be city centres, one each for the ex-boroughs of North York and Scarborough, in the north and east ends of the city respectively. The North York node includes a first-class concert hall and

adjacent theatre, miles from the city's main theatre district on Yonge and King Streets in the downtown. **39, 80, 85, 130**

Ottawa and the National Capital Region Ottawa is an Algonkian word, and refers to the Ottawa or Odawa nation that once lived around Michilimackinac and traded along the Ottawa River to Montreal. Immigrants from New England first settled the Ottawa area in 1800. The first industry of the Ottawa Valley was timber for export to Great Britain, followed some decades later by sawn lumber. These industries attracted further waves of immigrants – Irish and French Canadian, as well as military settlers, discharged army veterans of the Napoleonic Wars. The British army took a hand by constructing canals along the Ottawa River and then the Rideau Canal between the Ottawa and Lake Ontario. Bytown (named after Colonel John By, the supervising engineer) grew up around the entrance to the canal.

In 1854 Queen Victoria chose Bytown, which had been called 'a sub-Arctic lumber village,' to be the capital of the Province of Canada; it received the more dignified name of Ottawa. The provincial government erected a set of parliament buildings in the prevailing Gothic revival style in the mid-1860s. In 1867 Ottawa became the capital of the newly created Dominion of Canada.

Ottawa enjoys a uniquely beautiful setting, both natural and man-made: the Gatineau Hills (a national park)

Changing guard at the Canadian Parliament Buildings

across the river in Quebec, no fewer than four large rivers (the Ottawa, the Rideau, the Gatineau and the Lièvre) as well as the Rideau Canal which snakes through the city and is navigable by small craft. Much of the older part of the city (and many rural houses) was built in stone, and some of the government buildings, especially the Parliament Buildings (of which there are three, two from the 1860s, and one rebuilt with a tower after a fire in 1916) are impressive. Particularly noteworthy are the National Gallery (1988, designed by Moshe Safdie) and the Canadian Museum of Civilization (1989, designed by Douglas Cardinal).

Ottawa is in theory and in fact a bilingual city. Of the 325,000 in the city proper, (1 million is the population of the area on both sides of the Ottawa River) 25 per cent speak French as their usual language, and the remainder English. The federal government also imposed, starting in the 1960s, a bilingual requirement on frequently unwilling civil servants. The results have been mixed, but it is certain that French enjoys a considerably greater recognition and status in Ottawa than it once did.

To the north of the city, on the fringe of Gatineau National Park, is Kingsmere, the country estate of Mackenzie King, Canada's longest serving prime minister. The three houses of the estate are surrounded by lawns and trees, and by King's collection of 'romantic' ruins.

Next to Ulan Bator, Ottawa is the coldest national capital. The citizens have taken advantage of the fact by converting the Rideau Canal into the world's longest skating rink. Skiing is also popular on the low hills of the Gatineau; more challenging slopes are some distance away, in the Laurentian Hills north of Montreal. **43**

Niagara and Niagara Falls The Niagara Peninsula, between Lakes Ontario and Erie, is the garden of central Canada. Warmed by the lakes and sheltered by an escarpment that runs across southern Ontario and northern New York, the peninsula has a microclimate favourable to growing fruit and, especially, grapes. For many years Niagara was home to a lower-end wine industry whose products were at best undistinguished. In the 1970s and after, however, new varieties of grape were planted and the resulting wines began a slow and steady improvement. By concentrating on quality, the Niagara wine industry even survived the introduction of free trade with the United States and direct competition with abundant American wines.

The Canadian side of the Niagara River has for many years been subjected to strict government control, via a provincial parks commission. A parkway parallels the river from Fort George (restored to its appearance in 1800) **34** in the north to Fort Erie in the south (as reconstructed after the War of 1812). **34** Especially noteworthy are Niagara Falls, where the escarpment meets the Niagara River, Queenston Heights, the site of a

British victory in 1812, with a picturesque riverside village, and Niagara-on-the-Lake, home to a well-regarded summer drama festival devoted to the works of George Bernard Shaw. About 100 miles to the west is the rival and thriving Stratford (Ontario) Festival, devoted, naturally, to the works of William Shakespeare. Both festivals are open from May until (usually) October.

QUEBEC

Montreal, the Laurentians, and the Eastern Townships Human occupation of Montreal long predates the arrival of whites. Jacques Cartier, ascending the St Lawrence River in 1535, found an Iroquois village, Hochelaga, between a mountain (dubbed Mont Royal or Mount Royal) and the riverbank. Because of the Lachine Rapids, large ships could go no farther, so that when Montreal was eventually settled, in 1642, it became the inevitable transfer point between ships from Europe and canoes and small boats travelling inland. After its founding by the Sieur de Maisonneuve, Montreal became the centre of the fur trade. It grew slowly, behind a palisade, at risk from attacks by the Iroquois until the 1680s. In September 1760 the last French army in North America surrendered at Montreal to the British.

The British conquest brought with it an influx of fur traders from other British colonies, and, especially, from Scotland. Organized eventually as the North West Company, the traders laid a solid basis for the future prosperity of Montreal. The first bank, the Bank of Montreal, was established in 1817. In 1821, fur-trading money financed the founding of McGill University. Breweries, distilleries, and manufacturing of all kinds took root in Montreal. Irish immigration in the 1830s and 1840s turned Montreal into a predominantly English-language city, which it remained until the 1870s. Even afterwards, the business community, centred on St James Street (rue St-Jacques) long remained both English speaking and British in its habits and attitudes.

Montreal was the natural economic centre of the Dominion of Canada after 1867. It was the headquarters of the Grand Trunk and Canadian Pacific railways, the shipping hub of central Canada and the banking and financial centre. The massive head office of the Sun Life Assurance Company on Dominion Square downtown, still extant though converted to other uses, symbolized the power and achievements of English business. Waterpower from the rapids on the St Lawrence first powered mills and then electric utilities, which in turn ran a large manufacturing base in the city and then in its spreading suburbs. Montreal through the 19th century and most of the 20th was the largest city in Canada.

Although business was English, politics was increasingly French. French Canada did not join English Canada and the United States in imposing prohibition of alcohol in the 1920s, which meant that Montreal, alone of the large cities of the continent, retained a legal (and sometimes illegal) joie de vivre that outlasted even the disappearance of prohibition in the 1930s.

In the 1960s, Montreal, which was home to a thriving French Canadian intellectual community, naturally became a centre of separatist and radical ferment. At the same time, changes in the Canadian economy and in Quebec government policy undermined the English-language business community, which went into a long decline. When Quebec enacted restrictions on the use of English, as it did after 1973, the English decline accelerated. The Sun Life and Montreal's two largest banks moved to Toronto, and Montreal entered a period of stagnation. Two brilliant public entertainments, a world exposition, Expo '67, in 1967 and the Olympics in 1976, masked the stagnation. But the Olympics in particular left the city with a heavy debt as well as a beautiful but impractical stadium.

Montreal's mountain, Mont Royal, converted by the famous American landscape designer Frederick Law Olmstead into a spectacular park in the 19th century, dominates the city. Its Victorian business district is largely intact – of earlier buildings only the Château de Ramezay (1705), the French governor's residence, and the Bonsecours Church (1770) survive. The jewel among the city's churches is the Gothic Revival Eglise Notre-Dame (1823–29), with its stone facing and wooden interior; its dazzling blue and gold interior puts to shame the larger and more ornate but much duller Catholic and Anglican cathedrals.

Montreal in the 1960s developed a response to its harsh winter climate and scorching summers: an underground city of tunnels connecting major buildings such as Place Ville-Marie, the Place Bonaventure and the stock exchange, including some major hotels. A well-designed subway, the Metro, links the downtown to the suburbs, as far as the south shore of the St Lawrence.

Beyond the south shore, to the east, lie the Eastern Townships (Cantons de l'Est or Estrie) at the northern end of the Appalachians. Settled by immigrants from the United States early in the 19th century, the Eastern Townships remained an English-language bastion until World War II. Pockets are still English speaking, although the proportion of English-speakers has dropped precipitately. The architecture of the Townships is strikingly different from the rest of Quebec, and more closely resembles that of adjacent New England. **6, 13, 23, 38, 49–50, 51, 85, 117–8, 120–1, 130–1**

Quebec City and the Ile d'Orléans

The name Quebec is probably taken from the Algonkian, 'place where the river narrows.' It is an apt description: the St Lawrence narrows abruptly just in front of Quebec, and it was there that Samuel de Champlain in 1608 decided to locate his 'Habitation', the first permanent white settlement in New France. High cliffs flank the river, leaving a small space for a port and settlement – Lowertown in the

20th century; since the 18th century, most Quebeckers have lived in Uppertown, or 'the town above.'

Champlain was not the first settler or even the first visitor: there had been an Iroquois village, Stadacona, on the site, and Jacques Cartier had wintered there in 1535–36. Champlain's settlement grew slowly, and there was a major setback when the English captured Quebec in 1629. (It was returned in 1632.) Farming began on the flat land west of the city, and was extended to the alluvial Ile d'Orléans opposite the city in 1651. Quebec City was the seat of the government of New France, the residence of the governor and the bishop, and the principal port of the colony. Quebec fell to British forces in 1759 after a long siege (in which much of the city was reduced to rubble by British artillery) and a battle on the Plains of Abraham to the west of the city. (The British and French commanders, General James Wolfe and the Marquis de Montcalm, were both killed in the battle.) New France became the Province of Quebec, but Quebec City remained its capital, as it did for most of the time before the 1860s.

The British built elaborate fortifications around Quebec, making it a walled city with an elaborate star-shaped Citadel (1820–31); most of the walls and the Citadel are still extant. There was need for fortification: the Americans besieged the city, unsuccessfully, in 1775–76 and relations with the United States remained tense until some time after the War of 1812. Quebec was the principal port for the timber trade, supplying the Royal Navy with wood for its sailing ships, and attracted a large Irish immigrant population, many of whom settled in Sillery outside the walls to the west. (Many of the streets still bear Irish names.)

As railways replaced ships as the principal means of transport, Quebec lost importance as an economic centre, though it always retained a small manufacturing base. The departure of the British army from the Citadel in 1871 was also a loss, though the Canadian government always maintained its own small garrison in the place. As the seat of the provincial government after 1867 and as the home of what was for many years Quebec's only Catholic institution of higher learning, the Seminary (founded 1663), which expanded into Laval University in 1851, Quebec retained considerable importance.

Quebec remains Canada's only walled city, with impressive fortifications, including some walls from the French regime. The Citadel is one of the homes of Canada's governor-general and the base of the Royal 22nd Regiment, a French-speaking unit founded during World War I. Outside the Citadel's walls are several old sections of the city, characterized by stone houses dating back mostly to the early 19th century. The original Seminary buildings, dating in part from the 17th century and still following 17th-century design, are also located in Uppertown. An Anglican cathedral (1810) ministers to Quebec's tiny Anglican population. The Château Frontenac, a very large and elegant railway hotel, dominates Uppertown; a wooden boardwalk, Dufferin Terrace, extends along the cliff beside the hotel and along the Citadel walls, overlooking the river. Quebec's legislative buildings, a late 19th-century confection, sit beside the city wall; they house the province's National Assembly.

A funicular railway leads down the cliff to Lowertown, much of which has been painfully and expensively restored around the Place Royale. (Lowertown, like much of the city, had suffered extensive damage over time in repeated fires.)

East of the city there are the spectacular Montmorency Falls and a bridge to the Ile d'Orléans, which can also be reached by ferry from the city. The island is becoming somewhat suburbanized, but its villages retain much of their original character, stretching along the riverbank, centred on their 18th-century stone parish churches. **12–13, 14–15, 22, 23, 25–6, 30, 34, 35, 43**

Gaspé was predominantly but not exclusively French speaking and, like New Brunswick, divided between forest and fish in terms of industry. Gaspé is the northernmost end of the Appalachian Mountains, affording the region a rocky and hilly appearance. The beautiful seacoast, and especially the rock at Percé, attracts poets and painters and vacationers, making some of the coastal towns projections of folk art. **12**

THE TERRITORIES
North of the 60th parallel lie the 'territories' − from west to east

Yukon, the Northwest Territories and Nunavut. They are best compared to self-governing colonies: they have elections, legislatures, and cabinets, but they are not self-sustaining: the federal government pays most of their budgets and supervises their actions.

Yukon   The Yukon Territory covers 482,443 square kilometres and in 2000 had an estimated population of 30,343, more than half of whom live in the territorial capital, Whitehorse. The territory is mountainous interspersed with plateaus, topped off by a coastal plain along the Arctic Ocean. The climate is continental and can be severe: the lowest Canadian temperature ever recorded, $-63°C$, occurred at Snag in February 1947. On the other hand, temperatures in the summer can reach $35°C$ and the area around Whitehorse, in the south-west, is comparatively temperate. The area around Dawson is gold rush territory, site of the Klondike Gold Rush of 1898, and an effort has been made to preserve structures of the time and to recreate the atmosphere of the Gold Rush. The Yukon is also home to several of Canada's most notable national parks, especially Kluane (pronounced Kloo-wah-nee), established in 1972 and a UNESCO World Heritage Site. The park includes Mt. Logan, Canada's highest mountain (5959 m). **4, 7**

Northwest Territories (NWT)   The Northwest Territories go back to 1870, when they included all the land surrendered by the Hudson's Bay Company. They now cover only a fraction of their original surface, but are still, at 1,346,106 sq. km., a vast piece of land. The main geographical feature is the Mackenzie River, **5, 36** which stretches from Great Slave Lake to the Arctic Ocean, and its associated lakes – Great Slave and Great Bear. **5** The tree line and the Arctic Circle traverse Great Bear Lake, north of which the treeless tundra (sometimes called the Barren Grounds) stretches north to the ocean. This huge territory had only 42,056 people in 2000, concentrated in the south. Yellowknife, the territorial capital, has about 40% of the total population. The NWT has a number of national parks, of which the most accessible and perhaps the most spectacular is Nahanni along the South Nahanni River; it boasts a waterfall (Virginia Falls) twice the height of Niagara Falls. In 1978 it was named a UNESCO World Heritage Site, and is celebrated for canoeing and white-water rafting.

Nunavut   Established in 1999 out of the Northwest Territories, Nunavut has 27,340 inhabitants (85% Inuit) scattered over approximately 2,093,190 sq. km. Almost all of Nunavut lies north of the tree line – flat tundra, vast mountainous islands, with perpetual sun in summer and perpetual dark in winter. Nunavut has three national parks, two of which (Sirmilik and Auyuittuq) are notable for glaciers and are used for hiking, climbing and kayaking. **159**

Index

214 *Index*